特斯拉自传
被世界遗忘的天才

〔美〕尼古拉·特斯拉 著 徐萍 译

NIKOLA TESLA

北京理工大学出版社
BEIJING INSTITUTE OF TECHNOLOGY PRESS

版权专有 侵权必究

图书在版编目（CIP）数据

特斯拉自传：被世界遗忘的天才 /（美）尼古拉·特斯拉著；徐萍译. —北京：北京理工大学出版社，2020.6
　　ISBN 978-7-5682-8187-4

Ⅰ. ①特… Ⅱ. ①尼… ②徐… Ⅲ. ①特斯拉（Tesla, Nikola 1856–1943）—自传 Ⅳ. ①K837.126.1

中国版本图书馆CIP数据核字（2020）第035938号

出版发行 /	北京理工大学出版社有限责任公司
社　　址 /	北京市海淀区中关村南大街5号
邮　　编 /	100081
电　　话 /	（010）68914775（总编室）
	（010）82562903（教材售后服务热线）
	（010）68948351（其他图书服务热线）
网　　址 /	http://www.bitpress.com.cn
经　　销 /	全国各地新华书店
印　　刷 /	三河市冠宏印刷装订有限公司
开　　本 /	880毫米×1230毫米　1/32
印　　张 /	8.25
字　　数 /	140千字
版　　次 /	2020年6月第1版　2020年6月第1次印刷
定　　价 /	199.00元（全4册）

责任编辑 / 李慧智
文案编辑 / 李慧智
责任校对 / 刘亚男
责任印制 / 施胜娟

图书出现印装质量问题，请拨打售后服务热线，本社负责调换

目 录

第一章 我的早期生涯……………………………001

第二章 我在发明领域的最初努力………………021

第三章 后来的努力：旋转磁场的发现……………039

第四章 特斯拉线圈和变压器的发现………………057

第五章 不断放大的发射机的发明…………………073

第六章 遥控力学的艺术……………………………091

附录 尼古拉·特斯拉年谱…………………………117

My Inventions: Nikola Tesla's Autobiography ………121

I. My Early Life ……………………………………123

II. My First Efforts At Invention ………………145

III. My Later Endeavors: The Discovery of the Rotating Magnetic Field ……………………………………167

IV. The Discovery of the Tesla Coil and Transformer …187

V. The Magnifying Transmitter ……………………205

VI. The Art of Telautomatics ………………………227

第一章　我的早期生涯

人类的进步主要得益于技术上的创新，这是人类智慧最为重要的产物，其最终目标是在思想上完全掌控物质世界，并利用自然的力量来满足人类的需要。对于发明家来说，这是一项异常艰巨的任务，他们的工作常常被人误解，因此，他们的工作也得不到回报。但是，他们同时能够得到补偿，这一方面来源于他们对自身力量的激发，其过程令人愉悦；另一方面在于，他们知道自己是属于知识层面的特权阶级，如果没有他们，人类早就在与自然环境的残酷斗争中走向消亡。

至于我自己，已经充分享受了创造所带来的无限欢乐。多年以来，我的生活被这种快乐的享受所充斥着。如果把我的工作看成是一种劳动的话，那我认为自己是最勤奋的工人之一，除了睡眠以外的时间，我几乎都投身于工作之中。但是，如果对于工作的解释就是根据严苛的规则，在特定的时间里面，完成一项明确的任务,那么,我可能是最为游手好闲的人。每种强迫性的工作都需要牺牲生命的能量,而我从来没有付出过这样的代价。相反,我的成长依托于我的思想。

在这些文章中,我试图把自己的人生经历串连起来,进行实事求是的讲述。这一系列文章主要是写给那些年轻的读者的。虽然有些不情愿,但是我一定要详细地讲述我的年轻时代,讲述决定我职业生涯的环境和事件。

我们年少时期的努力纯粹是本能性的,完全受想象力的驱使,没有任何条条框框的限制和束缚。随着自身年龄的增长,理性不断加强,思维越来越系统化,对人生和工作越来越有规划。那些早期的冲动并没有立刻产生成效,但仍然堪称最伟大的时刻,有可能会塑造我们的命运。事实上,我到现在都有这样的感觉,如果我能够充分地挖掘和培养年少时期的冲动,而不是去压抑它们,我对世界将做出更为实用的贡献。但直到成年,我才意识到自己是一个发明家。

这是由一系列的原因所造成的。首先,我有一个哥哥,他是个极为罕见的天才,被上天赋予了特殊的才能——这是一种特殊的精神现象,即使生物学研究也无法对此进行解释。他的英年早逝使我的父母郁郁寡欢。

我们家曾经有一匹马,这是一位好朋友赠送的礼物,它属于阿拉伯品种,外表非常华丽,也很通人性,得到全家人的照顾和宠爱。有一次,它在非比寻常的危险情境之下救了我父亲的命。一个冬天的夜晚,有人通知我的父亲去执行一项紧急法事,在穿越山脉时,遇到了狼群。那匹马吓坏了,把我的父亲猛摔在地上,然后就跑开了。它回家的时候血流不止,也疲惫不堪,但在给我们发出警报的信号之后,马上就冲了出去,再一次回到了现场。在搜索队还没到来之前,它找到了我的父亲。我的父亲恢复了知觉,重新骑上马,却没有意识到自己已经在雪地里躺了几个小时。这匹马也是我哥哥受伤死亡的原因,我曾经见证了那个悲剧性的场面,尽管56年过去了,我的记忆却丝毫没有褪色。对哥哥成就的回忆,使我的每一次努力都显得相形见绌。

那时,对于我的父母来说,我所做的任何一件被人表扬和称颂的事情,只会徒增他们的痛苦,让他们更深切地感受到自己曾遭受的重大损失。所以,在成长的过程中,我一直极度缺乏自信。但是,没有人认为我是一个愚蠢的孩子,有一件事情令我印象深刻,这件事情也有助于让我理解别人对我的判断。一天,市参议员们经过了我和其他男孩们正在玩耍的街道。在这些受人尊敬的人群中,有一位最年长的、且非常富有的绅士,要给我们这些男孩子们每人一块银币。但是轮到我的时候,他突然停下来,并命令我说:"看着我的眼睛。"于是,我凝视着他的双眼,同时把手伸出去准备拿到那枚价值不菲的银币,然而令我感到失望的是,他说道:"不行,银币不多了,你什么也得不到,你实在是过于聪明了!"

过去,人们曾经讲述过一个关于我的故事,这个故事非常有趣。我有两位姑妈,她们都是满脸皱纹的老太太,其中一位的两颗牙齿是龅牙,如同象牙一样向外凸起。每次她亲吻我的时候,牙齿就会扎疼我的脸颊。最令我感到恐惧的莫过于这些充满慈爱的"丑"亲戚。有一次,在我很小的时候,妈妈抱着我,她们问我,两个姑姑谁比较漂亮,我仔细地观察她们的面孔,经过考虑之后,指着其中的一位说道:"她没有跟那一位一样丑陋。"

自从我出生,家里人就希望我长大后成为一名牧师,这令我极度苦恼。我渴望成为一名工程师,但是我的父亲非常古板,不同意我的选择。我的祖父是拿破仑军队中的一名军官,他的兄弟是数学教授,就职于一家著名的研究机构。父亲受到了军事方面的教育,但很奇怪,他却成了一名牧师,而且是一位威望极高的牧师。父亲是个博学的人,是真正的自然哲学家、诗人和作家。据说,他的布道可以与亚伯拉罕·阿·桑科塔·克拉拉相媲美。

他的记忆力超群,能够用不同的语言背诵大段的经典。他经常戏称,如果某些经典丢失,他可以凭借自己的记忆来对其进行恢复。他的写作风格也令人称道,遣词造句简短、明晰、睿智和幽默。他写的评论非常诙谐,独具特色,令人印象深刻。为了让人信服,我可以举一两个例子。

我家里雇用的人中,有一位名叫梅恩,他的眼睛是斜视的,主要在农场工作。一天,他在劈柴,我父亲就站在他附近。每当他举起斧子的时候,我的父亲就感到非常忐忑,于是父亲警告他说:"梅恩,拜托你看在上帝的面子上,不要砍向你所看到的东西,要砍向你意图击中的东西。"

另外一次,父亲驾车外出,一个朋友正好路过,他昂贵的毛皮大衣不小心剐蹭到了车轮上,我父亲这样提醒他:"拿好你的大衣,不要弄坏我的车轮。"

父亲还有一个非常奇怪的习惯,他喜欢自言自语,经常自己一人就能展开一场生动的对话,通过转换语调,变换角色,自我制造出一场激烈的辩论。偶然路过的人,一定会以为房间里面有好几个人。

尽管我所拥有的创造力主要是受到母亲的影响,但是父亲对我的训练同样颇有裨益。父亲对我的训练是多方面的,它包括猜测他人的想法，发现某种写作模式的不足，不断背诵长句，练习心算等。这些日常进行的训练，主要是为了强化我的记忆力，增强我的推理能力，特别是培养至关重要的批判能力，毫无疑问，这些能力的培养对我的成长产生了积极的影响。

我的母亲出生在农村，其家族古老绵远，有好几位发明家都是从这个家族诞生的。她的父亲和祖父发明了很多工具，以方便家里人进行家务劳动和农田耕作，也用于其他方面的劳作。她是一个真正伟大的女人，具有超于常人的技能、勇气和刚毅，她勇敢地面对生活中的风暴，拥有很多难忘的经历。她16岁的时候，一场致命的瘟疫席卷了整个乡村。她的父亲被叫走，给死者做最后的圣事。当父亲不在家的时候，她独自来到了邻居家里，给当时已经感染上重病的邻居提供帮助。邻居家中所有的5位成员相继死去。她给他们洗浴，换上衣服，按照乡村的习俗用鲜花来进行装饰，当她父亲回来的时候，发现母亲已经准备好了基督教葬礼所需要的一切。

我的母亲是顶级的发明家，如果她能更多地接触现代生活，能够抓住这种生活带来的众多机会，那么她会发明出更多的东西。她发明了各种各样的工具，安装了许多设备，运用她自己纺出的线，织出了带有精美图案的物品。她也进行播种和种植，并从植物中提取纤维。从黎明到深夜，她一直在工作，家里人的衣服、房间里的家具，大部分都是母亲的劳动成果。年过六旬的时候，她的手指仍然非常灵活，心灵手巧到甚至能够在眼睫毛上打三个结。

我的后知后觉还有另一个很重要的原因。少年时代，我遭受着非常痛苦的折磨，眼前经常浮现各种景象，往往还同时伴有强光的刺激，损害了我对真正物体的感知，困扰我的思想和行动。那些景象都是我曾经看到过的，不是我的主观想象。当有人跟我说起某个词汇的时候，这个单词所代表的物体就会生动地浮现在我的面前，以至于有时候我根本无法判断出，我看到的东西是真实的，还是虚幻的，这令我焦虑不安。我向心理学和哲学专业的学生们进行请教，但他们也无法对这样的现象做出令人满意的解释。这些现象看起来没有先例，但是我知道我的哥哥曾经面临相似的问题。最后，我自己得出的结论就是，当面临巨大刺激的时候，大脑对于视网膜产生了一种反射作用。这绝非疾病，亦非精神上遭受创伤所产生的幻觉。因为除此之外，我其他方面都很正常。为了让大家了解我的痛苦，可以想象一下：我看到一场葬礼，或者类似那样令人沮丧的场景。随后，在静谧的夜晚到来的时候，那些生动的场景就会清晰地呈现在我的面前，我竭尽所能也无法驱散它们。有时我试图用手驱散，但是毫无成效。如果我的解释成立，我们就可以把某人想象的任何物体投射到屏幕上，想象就变成了现实，就成了可以看到的东西。这样的进步将促使人们的关系发生革命性的变化。我确信，假以时日，这个奇迹一定能够实现。需要补充的一点是，对于如何解决这个问题，我已经思索了很多。

为了摆脱这些令人苦恼的景象，我试图把自己的注意力集中到我看到过的其他东西上面，通过这种方式，我会得到短暂的解脱。但是为了得到解脱，我需要不断地、像变魔术一般地构建出新的景象。不久，我就发现自己的所有"存储"都已经消耗殆尽，这是因为我缺乏对于世界的感知和视野——我所看到的物体或者是家里面的，或者是周边极为有限的环境里面的。当我第二次或者第三次进行这种脑力活动，追逐脑海中的影像，这种治疗手段就失效了。于是，受到本能的驱使，我会进行短途旅行，突破已知世界的障碍，这样我就看到了新的景观。最初，这些景象模糊不清，无法辨认，当我力图把注意力集中在这些景象上的时候，它们却一闪而过。随着时间的推移，我渐渐能够把它们组合在一起，其清晰度不断提高，最终呈现出来的就是一个真实的物体，形象非常明晰。我很快发现，只要我的视野越来越开阔，不断获得新的图景印象，我的精神就能够得到极大的抚慰。于是我就开始旅行，当然这是在脑海之中的旅行。每天晚上（有时也会在白天），当我孤身一人的时候，我就会踏上自己的旅程——看到新地方、新城市和新国家——我会居住在那里，遇见不同的人，与他们交朋友来收获友谊。令人难以置信的是，这些幻想中的人令我感到非常熟悉，就和现实生活中的人一样，他们的表现丝毫没有让我感到紧张。

于是，我经常采用这种模式来缓解自己的问题。一直到17岁，我的关注点转移到了发明创造上。令我感到欣喜异常的是，我能展开最充分的想象。我不需要任何的模型、绘图或者实验，就能够在头脑之中把这些东西清晰地呈现出来。于是，在不知不觉中，我已经构建出一种新的方法体系，能够把发明的理念直接付诸实践，而不需要纯粹的实验，依我之见，这种方法更迅捷，效率也更高。

当某个人试图把自己初步的想法付诸实践，并因此构造某项装置的时候，他总是无可避免地关注于装置的细节和缺陷。在他进行改善和重新构建的过程中，就会降低对于主要问题的注意力，并且忽略潜在的原则。这种方式最终也会取得成就，但往往以牺牲质量为前提。

我的方法则不然，我并不急于从事实际工作。当我有了初步的想法和思路，我首先会在头脑中构建相应的框架，然后在脑海里对该项装置不断进行调整、改善和操作。无论是在头脑中让涡轮机旋转，还是在车间里面进行测试，对我而言，这些都是非实质的，都是出自我的想象。我甚至能够想象出机器发生失衡的情形。无论过程如何，结果都是一致的。通过这种方式，我能够在不接触任何事物的情况下，快速地构建出设计框架，并且不断对其进行完善。当我把对该产品的所有细节想象完毕，并且看不出任何缺点的时候，我才把它付诸实践，实际制作出来的产品和我的想象毫无二致，实验步骤也和我的规划程序完全一致。20年的时间里，没有出现一次例外。为什么没有出现其他的情况呢？工程、电力和机械，几乎没有一门学科是无法用数学方法来进行处理的，其效果是由现有的理论和实际数据预先确定的。我坚持认为，把一个粗略的想法付诸实践，就是在浪费精力、金钱和时间。

我早年的痛苦还得到了另一种补偿。不断进行的脑力劳动开发了我的观察力，使我能够发现一个极为重要的事实。我注意到在非常特殊的、甚至是极为例外的条件下，图像的出现总是领先于实际的场景，而我则被迫把最初的推动力应用于其中。不久之后，这种努力就变成了自动行为，我能够轻松地把原因和结果联系起来。很快，我开始惊奇地意识到，我的每一个想法都受到外界映像的影响。不仅仅是这样一个案例，我的所有行动都以相似的方式被促进。在这段时间里，我很清楚地意识到，我只是一个被赋予了运动力量的机器，能够对感官的刺激做出反应，然后进行相应的思考，随后付诸行动。这一过程的实际结果，就是产生了遥控力学，当然，到目前为止，它还没有发展到十分完善的程度。但是，它的潜在力量终将展现出来。多年来，我一直在设计能够自我控制的"自动机器"，并相信一定可以生产出这样的装置，在一定程度上，它将在许多商业和工业部门产生革命性的影响。

大约在我12岁的那一年，我第一次成功地把影像从我的脑海里面驱逐了出去，当然这是付出很大努力才得以实现的，但是对于我曾经提到过的强光闪烁这一问题，我却无能为力，更无法控制。这是我一生中最奇怪的体验，是令人费解之谜。强光的出现也是有规律的，通常是在我处于危险境地、陷入痛苦情绪或者极度兴奋的状态时才会发生。有时候，我甚至能够看到周围的空气在燃烧。光的强度并没有随着时间推移而逐渐弱化，反而呈现出不断强化的态势，在我25岁的时候达到了顶峰。

1883年，当时我生活在巴黎，一位非常著名的法国制造商向我发出了一份邀请，让我跟他一起去打猎，我接受了邀请。长期以来，我一直在工厂里面生活和工作，这次打猎呼吸到新鲜空气令我感到精力充沛。但是在我回到城市之后的当晚，我就看到了一束强光，就像脑袋里面有一个小太阳一样。于是整个夜晚，我都在对我那颗饱受困扰的脑袋进行冷敷。最终，强光出现的频率在逐渐减少，力度也在逐步减弱，最终完全平息是在3个星期之后。当他第二次对我发出邀请的时候，我只能用不容置疑的语气来回答："不！"

这种发光的现象仍然不时地出现在我的脑海里面，尤其是当我有了新观点的时候。但是这些强光不再令人感到兴奋，其力度也在逐渐减弱。当我紧闭双眼，首先呈现出来的是均衡的深蓝色背景，但与晴朗、没有星星的夜晚的天空并不一样。几秒钟的时间里，场景就发生了变化，充满了无数个绿色的闪耀的雪花，它们分成几层，向我的方向奔来。然后，在右侧就会出现两个平行的美丽图案，还有间距非常短的线条，图形和直线呈直角关系，颜色五彩缤纷，主要是黄绿色和金色。不久之后，这些线条变得愈加明亮起来，整个场景上面都是不断闪烁的光点。在我的视野之内，这幅图片缓慢移动，10秒钟之后，在左侧消失，留下的是一幅令人不悦又呆板的灰色，但是很快它们就变成了波涛汹涌的云海，试图把自己塑造成非常生动的形状。令人感到奇怪的是，我无法把这种灰色转换成为具体的构思，直到第二个阶段开始到来。每一次入睡之前，我的眼前都会飞快地掠过人和物体的影像。当我看到这些影像的时候，我就知道自己将要失去意识，进入梦乡。如果影像没有出现，那就意味着这是一个失眠的夜晚。

为了说明在我的早期生涯中，想象力究竟发挥了多大的影响，我需要用另一个古怪的经历来对此加以印证。我像大多数孩子那样，也喜欢跳跃，并且我有一种强烈的愿望——希望空气能够把我支撑起来。偶尔会出现这样的情况，山区吹来强劲且富含氧气的风，我的身体就如同软木一样轻轻地在空中飘浮，并会持续很长的时间。这种经历令人非常愉悦，但是当我醒悟过来时，我又感到非常失望，因为这完全是我的主观臆想。

在那段时期里面，我有了很多古怪的喜好和厌恶以及习惯，它们的养成部分是由于外界环境的影响，但有些的确让人无法理解。我对女人佩戴耳环的行为感到极其厌恶，但是如果她们佩戴其他的饰品，比如说手镯之类，多少会让我感到愉悦，当然这也取决于首饰的设计感。珍珠材质的饰品会让我感觉不舒服，但是我却迷恋于水晶的光泽，以及带有尖锐边缘和平面的东西。我不会触摸任何一个人的头发,除非有人拿着左轮手枪对准我强迫我这样做。只要看到桃子,我就会发烧。如果房间里有一小片樟脑,无论它被放置在哪里,我都会感到特别不舒服。直到现在,我对这些令人不快的东西仍然非常敏感。当我把小的正方形纸片放在盛满液体的盘子里面时,我的嘴里就会感到特别恶心。走路的时候,我会数着步数;吃饭的时候,我会计算出汤盘的容积、咖啡杯的容积和食物的份数,否则我这餐饭对于我来说就毫无趣味。我所有做过的事情必须是3的倍数,否则我就会重复去做,即使花费几个小时也在所不惜。

一直到8岁的时候,我的性格还非常软弱,非常优柔寡断。我既没有勇气,也没有能力去做出果断的决定。我的情绪起伏不定,就像海里波浪的涌动一样,而且经常在两个极端之间永无休止地变来变去。我的愿望过多,它一直在消耗我的力量,而且就像九头蛇的头部一样,呈倍数增长。我被对于生活、死亡和宗教恐惧的痛苦想法所困扰。我非常迷信,特别害怕出现邪恶幽灵、鬼怪、食人魔和其他怪物。然后,突然在某一时刻,我的性格发生了巨大转变,从而改变了我整个的人生轨迹。

在所有的物品之中,我最为热爱的就是书籍。家里有一个很大的书房,父亲拥有很多的藏书。只要有可能,我就会读书,尽量满足自己的阅读热情。父亲不允许我这样做，当他发现我翻阅他书籍的时候，就会大动肝火。一旦他发现我在偷偷阅读，他就会把蜡烛藏起来，不想让读书损害我的视力。但是，我找到了牛脂，用它制作出了灯芯，把它们放在锡制的容器之中，作为照明使用。每当夜晚来临，我都会把书房的锁眼和缝隙堵上，然后阅读到黎明时分，那时所有的人还在梦乡之中，只有母亲已经起床开始了烦琐的日常工作。

有一次，我偶然翻到了一本小说，名字叫《阿巴菲》（又名《阿巴的儿子》），作者是著名的匈牙利作家约西卡，我读到的是塞尔维亚语的译本。这本书唤醒了我隐匿的力量，我开始有意识地进行自我控制。最初的时候，我的决心很快就烟消云散，就像四月的雪会快速融化一样。但是我逐渐战胜了自己的弱点，感觉到了以前从未体验过的快乐——这是遵循自己意愿做事所带来的快乐。

在这段时间里，这种大量的头脑锻炼成了我的第二天性。刚开始的时候，我的愿望还处于被压制的状态，但是我的愿望和意志逐渐趋同。持续进行了几年的训练之后，我已经能够控制自己，能够对自己的情绪收放自如，而这种情绪甚至会对最强壮的人构成毁灭性的打击。有一个年龄段，我疯狂地迷恋上了赌博，我的父母为此非常苦恼。那时的我，在坐下来玩纸牌游戏时，会感觉到非常的快乐和享受。我的父亲一直过着榜样般的生活，不能原谅我如此放任地浪费时间和金钱。我有坚定的决心，但是我的人生哲学却非常糟糕。我对他说："只要我下定决心，我随时都可以停止下来，但是让我放弃犹如生活在天堂里面的快乐，这是否值得呢？"父亲在很多场合，都会表达对我的愤怒和轻蔑之情，但是我的母亲却没有这样做。她非常了解男人的本性，明白一个人只有通过自身的不断努力，才能够实现自我救赎。某一天下午，我打牌的时候输掉了身上所有的钱，并准备再赌一场，但是却苦于没有筹码。正在这时，我的母亲走到我身边，拿着一沓钱递给我说："去吧，好好享受！你越早输掉我们所拥有的一切，你就越能够克服这个弱点，我知道你一定会做到的。"她是正确的，我战胜了自己。我唯一感到遗憾的就是，那种欲望的强度再加大100倍就更好了。我不仅征服了自己赌博的愿望，而且彻底地把它从心中驱逐出去，没有留下任何一点点的残余。从那之后，我丧失了对于任何赌博的兴趣，就像把坏牙剔除一样的彻底。

还有一个时期，我吸烟无度，它甚至威胁到了我的健康。随后，我调度起自己的意志力，成功地戒除了烟瘾，而且再也没有复发过。很久前，我的心脏不太舒服，后来发现是因为我每天早晨喝咖啡。虽然很艰难，但我还是立即放弃了喝咖啡的习惯。就这样，通过坚定的意志力，我逐渐战胜了所有其他的不良习惯。这不仅保住了自己的生命，而且从大多数人所认为的匮乏和牺牲中获得了巨大的满足感。

在完成理工学院和大学的课程之后，我一度陷入了精神崩溃的困境。其间，我观察到了许多现象，它们非常奇怪，许多人对此表示难以置信。

第二章 我在发明领域的最初努力

我将简短地叙述一下我这些年里的非凡经历，这主要是出于两方面的原因：一方面，心理学和生理学专业的学生们可能对此抱有一定的研究兴趣；另一方面，这段时期的痛苦经历对我的心智发展产生了至关重要的影响，也影响了我随后的工作。但在讲述之前，我将要介绍一下相关的环境和条件，这有助于解释这些经历。

从很小的时候开始，我的父母就教育我要把精力集中在自己的身上，要求我不断地进行自我反省。对于年幼的我来说，这是一件很痛苦的事情；但是随着年龄的增长，我的观念发生了转变，这也许就是因祸得福，因为这种方式教会我在生活之中去欣赏内省的不可估量的价值，而自省也是人生获得成功的必要手段。现今社会的信息量庞大，源源不断地涌入我们的脑海之中，实际上这在很多方面都是非常有害的。很多人沉迷于外部世界的诱惑，而完全没有意识到自己内心的真正需要。数百万人的英年早逝都与此息息相关。即使那些一直在进行运动健身的人，也常犯一个错误，就是忽视想象力的作用，从而忽视了真正的危险。对某个人是真实的东西，也或多或少地适用于人群整体。

下面，我通过禁酒运动进行一下解释。虽然饮酒并不违宪，但是这个国家正在采取严厉的措施禁止饮酒，由此带来的影响就是人们开始迷恋于咖啡、茶、香烟、口香糖和其他比较刺激性的东西，甚至从青少年时期就已经沉迷于此，刺激性的物品对于国民体质损害很大，这可以从他们的身体素质上看出来。举个例子，在我的学生时代，我收集了维也纳出版的《咖啡者之家》提供的资料，死于心脏疾病的人数有时占据死亡总数的67%。我们也可以在过度饮茶的城市进行类似的观察。这些美味的饮料让人兴奋不已，逐渐耗尽了脑细胞。它们同样严重影响动脉循环，只不过其影响发展比较缓慢，起初并不容易让人察觉。另一方面，烟草让人在思考的时候感到放松，似乎减轻了人的劳动强度，能够让头脑进行更有活力的思考。嚼口香糖让身体感觉到短暂的舒适，但它很快就会耗尽腺体系统，造成无法弥补的损害，更不用说它最终给人所带来的那种厌恶感。

少量的酒精是一种很好的补品，但是大量饮用就会导致中毒，这种影响是无形的，无论它是作为威士忌被摄入，还是在胃里面消耗糖分都是如此。不应该忽视的是，这些刺激性物品都是消耗者，就像它们所做的那样，在遵循着严格的适者生存法则。那些意图改革的人应该意识到人类永恒的邪恶之处，这使得冷漠的自由放任要比强制性的限制要好很多。事实是，在现有的条件下，为了做好工作，我们需要刺激性的东西，为此，我们必须有意识地节制自己，在每一个领域控制我们的愿望。这就是我几十年如一日在做的事情，通过这种方式，我的身心都非常年轻。

禁欲非我所愿，但是这种经历带给我丰厚的回报。为了让人信服，我给大家讲述一下我亲身经历的两件事情。

不久之前的一个略显寒冷的夜晚，我正在返回宾馆的路上，地面有些滑，路上也没有出租车。距离我身后大约半个街区的地方，一个男人也在匆忙赶路，估计也是想早点回到温暖的住处。突然，我的脚下一滑，双腿随即腾空，几乎就在同时，我的脑海里一闪念，紧接着神经做出了迅速反应，肌肉随即收紧，身体旋转180度，双手撑地。随后，我就像什么事情都没有发生过一样，继续赶路。那个陌生人追上了我。

"您多大年龄了？"他问道，并仔细地打量着我。

我回答说："59岁了，你怎么问起这个？"

他非常惊讶地说道:"我曾经看到过猫这样做,但是从来没有想到人也可以。"

一个月之前,我想换一副眼镜,定制一副新的,为此来到眼科医生那里进行常规的配镜检查。当我轻而易举地在特定的距离读出了视力表上最小的数字,他难以置信地看了我很久,而当我告诉他我已经60岁的时候,他更是大吃一惊。我的朋友经常评价我穿的衣服都非常合身,就像戴的手套那样,但是他们不会想到我的衣服几乎都是35年之前的尺寸,从来没有变过。35年来,我的体重也毫无变化。

关于我的体重,有一个非常有趣的故事。1885年冬天的某个夜晚,爱迪生先生,爱德华·H.约翰逊(爱迪生照明公司的总裁)先生,巴特尔先生(该公司的经理),还有我,走入了第福斯大道65号(公司所在地)对面的一个小地方。有人建议做个猜测体重的游戏。首先是猜测我的体重,爱迪生摸了我的全身之后,给出的结论是:"特斯拉的体重是152磅,丝毫不差。"他说得对极了。当时,我的净重是142磅,一直保持到现在。我轻轻地问约翰逊先生:"太神奇了,爱迪生怎么会猜出我的体重,而且还如此准确?"

他小声回答说:"哦,你不知道吧,我告诉你啊,但是这件事情一定要保密,不要对任何人说起。他曾经在芝加哥的屠宰场工作过很长一段时间,每天都要给成千上万头猪称重!这就是原因之所在!"

我的朋友洪·昌西·M.迪普,曾经讲过一个英国人的故事,昌西给他讲了自己原来的奇闻异事,这位英国人的表情是困惑不解的,他丝毫没有理解昌西的故事,直到一年之后,才明白故事的真谛,并开口大笑起来。在这里,我也要坦率地承认,刚开始我也没有理解约翰逊的诙谐语言,很久之后我才明白其中的幽默之处。

目前,我身心健康,生活幸福,这完全是因为我非常注意自己的生活方式。最令人震惊的事情,是我在年轻的时候曾经三次被病魔打倒,情况非常严峻,甚至医生对我的康复都不抱有任何希望。不仅如此,由于无知和放任,我遇到了各种各样的困难、危险和伤害,但是后来都轻松化解,就如同遇到了魔法一般。我多次差点儿被淹死,差点儿被活活煮死,也差一点儿就被送进了火葬场。我差一点儿被活埋,被冻死,也差一点儿被丢弃。我曾经从疯狗、野猪和其他野兽的口下死里逃生。我经历过可怕的疾病的打击,遇到过各种各样稀奇古怪的天灾人祸。今天的我老当益壮,精力充沛,似乎是个奇迹。但当我回想起这些事件时,我确信神灵对我的保护并不是偶然的。

  发明家的辛勤工作，本质上就是为了救助生命。无论他是在控制能量，改善装置，抑或在创造新的舒服和便利的设施，他的工作都是在增加我们存在的安全感。相对于普通的个体而言，在面临危险的时候，他能够更好地保护自己，因为他善于观察，应变能力很强。虽然我没有更多的证据表明我自己也具备这样的特征，但是大家可以通过我的个人经历看出这一点。现在我举两个例子，读者们可以自己进行判断。

  一个例子是我14岁的时候，有一次，我和朋友们一起游泳，我想吓唬一下他们。我的设想是，我藏身于一个漂浮着的物体下面，然后从物体的另一个端点那里冒出来。我擅长游泳和潜水，就像鸭子一样能够随意纵横于水面，所以我有充分的自信可以玩好这个游戏。于是，我一头扎进水里，脱离了小伙伴们的视线，转身快速地向另一个方向游过去。我一直坚信在这个漂浮的物体下面我是安全的。当我想浮出水面的时候，令我大失所望的是，我的头碰到了一根横梁。很快，我再次潜入水中，继续向前游去，直到我气喘不止，于是我第二次准备浮出水面，但是我的脑袋再一次又撞到了横梁。我开始感到绝望。但是，我很快集中全身的力量，做了第三次疯狂的尝试，然而结果是一样的。窒息的感觉越来越强烈,变得让人无法忍受,我的头脑变得晕晕乎乎,感觉自己在不断下沉。那时,我的处境让人绝望,突然我的脑海里强光一闪,漂浮物的构造呈现在我的面前,我好像突然辨别出来水面和横梁上的木板之间有个空隙,于是在即将失去意识之前,我漂浮上来,把我的嘴巴贴近木板,准备呼吸一点空气,很不幸的是,空气连同水浪一起进入我的嘴里面,我几乎被呛死。有好几次,都是这样的过程,我犹如身处梦境之中,直到我的心脏从狂跳趋于平静,我才开始镇定下来。随后,我又开始潜入水下,也没有成功,我在水里完全迷失了方向,但是。最后我成功地浮出了水面。当时,我的朋友们对我的生还已经不抱有任何的希望,他们正在寻找我的尸体。

那本是一个最佳的游泳季节,但是由于我的鲁莽冲动,完全失去了它应有的乐趣。然而,我很快就忘记了这次的教训,两年之后,我陷入了更糟糕的一种境地。在我上学的时候,我学习的城市旁边有一条河流,那里有一座大型面粉厂的水坝横跨河流。平时,河水的深度只超过大坝2~3英寸[①],在河里游泳没有任何危险,纯粹属于锻炼行为,我经常去锻炼,且乐此不疲。一天,

---

① 1英寸=2.54厘米。

我独自来到河边，像往常一样快乐地游泳。但是，当我距离那个石头建筑的大坝很近的时候，突然发现河水的高度已经上涨了，我被卷入了水流之中。我试着逃离，但已经来不及了。非常幸运的一点是，我用双手抓住了墙壁。我的胸腔承受着巨大的压力，头部勉强露出水面。周围什么人都没有，我的声音也被掩埋在水的咆哮声中。慢慢地，我变得筋疲力尽，几乎无法支撑自己。当我将要放弃，就要掉到底下的岩石上面的时候，我的脑海里面又出现了一道强光，这是一个我非常熟悉的图表，上面呈现出关于水压的原理，运动中的水流压力与受力面积成正比例关系，于是，我转向左侧，神奇的一幕发生了，压力减轻了，而且身处这样的位置，似乎更能够抵御水流的力量。但是，我仍然身处危险的境地，如果我得不到及时的帮助，早晚还是会被冲入水中。现在，我的双手比较灵活，但是我的右手几乎没有什么力气，只有左手还能够坚持。正因为如此，我也不能换位休息，除了把身体慢慢地沿着大坝移动，我什么都做不了。当时我的脸面对着面粉厂的方向，我必须改变自己的姿势，因为那里水流湍急，水也很深。这是个漫长而痛苦的过程，几乎要失败了，快到堤坝的时候几乎已经无法承受。我耗尽全身的力气，终于昏倒在岸边。我左侧的皮肤几乎全面撕裂，发起了高烧，病程持续了几个星期的时间。这样的经历还有很多，我选取了两个介绍给你们，只是想说明，若非发明家自身具有的本能，我早已经丧生，无法活到现在给你们讲这两个故事。

那些对我和我的发明有兴趣的人经常向我发问，我是什么时间开始发明创造的，是怎样开始发明创造的。对此，我的记忆非常模糊，只能根据大概的记忆来进行回答。我在第一次进行发明的时候，充满了雄心壮志，当时发明的是一种装置及其使用方法。对于前者，我是进行改进，对于后者，那完全是我的首创。发明的经过是这样的。平时经常跟我在一起玩的一个玩伴，突然得到了一套钓鱼用的鱼钩和钓具，整个村庄的人都为此感到激动不已。第二天凌晨，全村的人都出动了，跟着他一起去抓青蛙。我被留下了，备感孤立，原因在于不久前我和这个玩伴吵了一架。我在生活中从来没有看到过鱼钩的模样，在我的想象里，钓钩非常精美，品质也非常独特，所以没能去参加集体活动，我感到非常的懊恼。突然，我灵机一动，决定自己尝试一下，于是，我找到了一段非常软的铁丝和两块石头，把铁丝两端凿成特别发尖的形状，然后折弯它，把它绑在一条非常结实的绳子上面。随后，我砍断了一根棒子，收集到一些鱼饵，来到小河边，找到了一处青蛙密集之处。但是很长的时间我都一无所获，令我灰心丧气。突然，摇摇晃晃的钓钩前面出现了一只青蛙，它蹲坐在树桩之上。起初，它的状态看起来非常不好，眼睛凸出来，充满了血丝，很快，它的身体膨胀起来，相当于其正常尺寸的2倍，随即它猛扑过来咬住了鱼钩。我立即拉起鱼钩捉住了它。此后，我一直都在用这个方法捕捉青蛙，都非常成功。而我的那些小伙伴们，虽然有着装备良好的器械，却一无所获。他们看到我的战绩，嫉妒得要命。很长的一段时间里，我都对此保密，它成为我的垄断性技术，一直到圣诞节，我才把它公之于众。于是，所有的男孩都学会了这项技术，第二年夏天，附近的青蛙们都难逃厄运。

在接下来的另一次尝试中，我似乎是在本能的驱使下进行的行动，这在后来一直指引着我的发明——即充分利用大自然的能量来为人类提供服务。这次实验的对象是五月的金龟子（在美国它被称为六月虫），它是一种名副其实的害虫，有时仅仅凭借其身体的重量就能够把树枝压断，它们甚至能够把灌木丛染成黑色。我的做法是这样的：把四只虫子固定在一个横木之上，把横木放置在细细的轴上面，然后把它们固定在一个大的圆盘上面，于是就可以得到很大的"力量"。这些虫子充满活力，一旦开始旋转，就不会停下来，就会连续旋转，天气越热，它们的动作幅度就越大。这一切进展得非常顺利,却突然被打断了,一个男孩来到了我进行试验的地方,他是奥地利军队一个退休军官的儿子。这个淘气鬼竟然吃掉了活生生的虫子,吃的样子就像在享受美味,看起来就像在吃小牡蛎一样。那个画面太让人恶心了,于是我丧失了把实验进行下去的热情,也因为这个原因,此后我再也无法触摸五月的金龟子,甚至也不敢触碰其他的虫子。

我印象之中,在那之后,我进行的工作是拆散和组装祖父的钟表。在拆散的这个阶段,我进行得非常顺利,但是组装阶段总是遇到困难。所以祖父生气了,中断了我的工作,直到30年之后,我才得以组装另一块钟表。

不久之后,我又开始制作流行的枪支,其组件包括一个空心管,一个活塞,两个充满麻类植物的栓塞。开枪的时候,活塞被迅速冲击到枪体的中央,带有手把的管子被推向后方。两个栓塞之间的空气遭到挤压,温度急剧升高,其中一个就会发射出去,声音很大。这项技术要求从空心的杆子中选择一个合适的具有一定锥度的管子。我做得非常成功,但是由于它打碎了家里的玻璃,所以遭到了家人的干预。

如果我的记忆力比较准确的话,我当时还从家具上找到木条,用来刻剑,因为家具上的木头唾手可得。那时,我深受塞尔维亚民族诗歌的影响，充满了对于英雄业绩的钦佩之情。我把玉米秸秆想象成敌人，常常以宝剑作为武器，与它们展开几个小时的厮杀和作战。我毁坏了庄稼，我的妈妈经常为此打我的屁股。而且，这是实实在在的惩罚。

　　上面讲的故事，都发生在我6岁以前。小学一年级之前，我们家一直住在史密里安村，那也是我出生的地方。之后，我们家搬到了附近的戈斯皮奇小城。住所的变化对我而言就像是一场灾难。从此，我伤心地与猪、鸡、羊和成群的鹅分离，我常常想象它们每天伴着太阳早起，日落时分从觅食场所归来的情景，其排列井然有序，非常完美，甚至堪称最好的飞行员中队。而在我们的新房子里面，我就像被囚禁起来一样，只能通过百叶窗观察外面陌生的行人。我非常羞涩，不愿意面对生人，我宁愿面对一只凶猛的狮子，也不愿意看到在街上游荡的纨绔子弟。对我最为艰难的考验发生在星期日，我必须正装出席，参与教会活动。在那里，我遇到了一场意外，多年后回想起来，它仍然令我的血液凝固如酸奶一般。这是我在教堂里的第二次危险经历。很久以前，我被困在一座古老的小教堂里，那座教堂位于一座人迹罕至的山上，每年游人只有一次上山的机会。那次经历非常可怕，但是这次则更为糟糕。

镇子里面有一位非常有钱的女人，她人品不错，就是有些虚荣，讲究排场。她去教堂的时候，都是浓妆艳抹，穿着有很长裙裾的衣服，还带着一堆仆人。一个星期天，刚刚敲响钟声，我就冲下了楼梯，这位夫人刚好经过，我踩到了她巨大的裙裾，只听到撕拉一声，听起来就像新兵步枪开火的声音，夫人的裙摆裂开了。我父亲非常生气，轻轻地打了我一记耳光，这是他唯一打我的一次，但是时至今日我甚至都能够感到脸上的疼痛。当时我的尴尬和困惑，几乎无以言表。之后，我几乎被孤立排斥，直到另外一件事情的发生，我才得到了救赎。

一位特别有进取心的年轻人，组织了一个消防队，购买了新的消防装置，提供制服，组织队员展开训练，准备游行仪式。消防队一共有16个人，消防车被涂成红黑相间的颜色，非常漂亮。一天下午，正式的表演开始了，消防装置被运送到河边。全镇上的人都出动了，来见证这一伟大的奇迹。当演讲和仪式进行完毕之后，该进行水泵喷水表演了，但是喷嘴里一滴水都没有喷出来。现场所有的专家和教授试图找出问题的所在，但是一无所获。我到现场的时候，人们已经放弃了希望。我以前丝毫也不了解这个机器，对于空气压力也一无所知，但是出于本能，我觉得是水下的出水管发生了故障，最后发现的确如此。于是，我蹚水工作了一会儿，连上了水管，后来打开水管的时候，水流喷涌而出，有几个人的节日礼服都被打湿了。阿基米德曾经在锡拉丘兹的大街上裸奔，声嘶力竭地喊道："找到了！"但是我的这次经历留下了更深刻的印象，我被人们扛在肩膀之上，成了当天的英雄。

在城里安顿下来后，我在所谓的师范学校开始了为期四年的学业，这为以后我在学院真正的实践学习打下了重要的基础。在这期间，我孩子气的壮举和麻烦，都在继续出现。在其他的事情上，我也非常特别。我有一个奇怪的绰号——捕捉乌鸦的冠军。我所使用的方法简单易行。我来到森林里面，藏身于灌木丛之间，模仿鸟鸣的声音。有时，我会听到几声应答，很快，乌鸦就会扑向我身边的灌木丛。随后，我需要做的就是扔出一块纸板，分散乌鸦的注意力，然后在它跳出灌木丛之前，跳起来抓住它。通过这种方法，我抓住了很多的乌鸦。但是有一次，一件事情的发生，使得我对乌鸦产生了敬意。我曾经捉住了一对很漂亮的乌鸦，然后和朋友一起回家。当我们离开树林的时候，成千上万只乌鸦聚集在一起，发出了可怕的声音。仅仅用了几分钟的时间，它们就追赶上了我们，把我们围在中间。突然，我的后脑上遭受到打击，我摔倒在地上，它们继续恶狠狠地攻击我。我被迫释放了那一对乌鸦，然后跑到我朋友避难的山洞里面。

在学校的教室里面，有一些机械模型，令我产生了浓厚的兴趣，于是我的注意力发生了转移，转移到了水力涡轮机上面。我制作了很多这样的机械，并从中获得了极大的乐趣。我非凡的人生经历，很多时候是偶然性造就出来的。我的叔叔认为这种爱好毫无用处，完全是在浪费时间，曾经多次批评我。我曾经迷恋于书中关于尼加拉瓜瀑布的描述，并在脑海之中展开了想象，瀑布的水流推动着巨大的水轮进行旋转。我告诉叔叔，我将来要去美国，把这个构想付诸实践。30年之后，我的想法在尼加拉瓜瀑布变成了现实，想象的力量是无穷的，令人难以置信。

我还有很多各种各样的发明，其中最为突出的就是劲弩。箭头射出去之后，很快就能从视野中消失，即使在很近的距离，也能穿透厚度为1英寸的松木。随着弓的不断收紧，我腹部的皮肤变得像鳄鱼皮一样，我经常在想是不是因为这个原因，我现在甚至可以消化鹅卵石！

同时，我也不想保守秘密，我能够进行投掷表演，即使回到古希腊的竞技场上我也会表演得毫不逊色。现在，我要讲述自己的一个壮举，是关于投掷的故事，读者们肯定会觉得惊讶不已。当时，我和叔叔正在河边漫步。太阳即将落山，鳟鱼很顽皮，时不时地会有一只鳟鱼飞到空中，它那闪闪发光的身体，在身后岩石的衬托下，轮廓非常分明。在这种非常有利的环境下，可能任何一个男孩都会击中这条鳟鱼，但是我给自己设计了比较高难的目标，我预先告诉叔叔，一定要观察我击打鱼的细节。我要用石头击打，让它撞击在岩石上面，而且分成两截。我说到做到，叔叔看着我，吓得魂不附体，高声喊叫："你是个魔鬼，滚开！"之后有好几天，他都没有和我说话。当然还有其他的记录，尽管也有突出之处，但我感觉与这些相比都黯然失色，现有的这些已经足够让我在上千年的时光里面进行回味了。

第三章 后来的努力：旋转磁场的发现

10岁的时候,我进入一所真正的实科中学,这所中学是新建立的,设施非常完备。在物理教研室,配置了各式不同的、经典的电力和机械设备。教师们不时地进行演示和实验,这令我着迷,它对于我从事发明研究是一个很强的刺激。我对数学也抱有极大的学习热情,因为杰出的速算能力,我经常得到老师的表扬,这是因为我超强的想象力,并且得到了进行运算的设备,这次我没有采用通常的那种直觉方式,而是在进行实实在在的运算。无论数字达到多么复杂的程度,对我来讲原理都是一样的。而且,无论我在黑板上写下这些象征性的符号也好,还是在脑海中把它们连接起来也罢,结果都是一样的。但是在学校中,也有我非常不喜欢的科目,那就是徒手画的课程。这门课一上就是几个小时,令我难以忍受。这一点并不符合我的家风,因为我家里的大部分成员都非常擅长徒手画。我之所以厌恶这门课程,可能仅仅是因为我的偏好是不受打扰地思考。如果不是有几个特别笨的孩子完全不务正业，我这门课程的成绩应该就是最差的。在当时的教育体制之下，这是一个很大的缺憾，将会危及我的整个学习生涯，所以父亲几经周折，把我从一个班级转向另一个班级。

在第二学年，我开始沉迷于另一种想法——通过稳定的气压产生持续的运动能量。我在上一章讲述过的消防车的水泵事故激发了我丰富的想象力，使我很早就意识到真空的巨大能量。我的愿望开始膨胀，渴望驾驭这种取之不竭的能量，在相当长的时间里，我没有取得任何突破。但是，我最终的努力通过一项发明得以具体化，使我取得了超越他人的成就。

想象一个圆柱体在两个轴承上自由旋转，柱体的一部分被一个矩形槽包围，槽的开口处被一个隔板封闭，圆柱体也因此被分割成两个部分，中间是气密式滑动的接头。两部分之中有一部分是密封的，一旦气体被全部释放出来，那么另外一个就会打开，于是就出现了一个永久旋转的圆柱体。我一直都是这么设计和考虑的。我根据这个设想用木头打造了一个模型，经过仔细琢磨，把气泵安在一边，而且确实观察到旋转的倾向，我兴奋异常。

我想完成的另一件事情，就是机械飞行，虽然我曾经有过非常令人沮丧的经历，那次我手拿一把雨伞，从房顶上跳下来，结果可想而知。过去我一直在思考的一件事情就是，通过空中之旅把自己带到很远的地方，但是苦于没有路径实现这一目标。但是，现在我有了一些具体的想法，制作一个飞行器，结构非常简单，只需要旋转的轴承，扑翼的翅膀，还有就是真空的无限力量。从那时起，我每天的愿望似乎就是享受舒适豪华的空中之旅，待遇似乎如同所罗门国王一样。多年之后，我才明白一件事，空气的压力只有垂直于圆柱体的表面才能够发挥出作用，我观察到的那种轻微的旋转作用，其原因在于漏气。我是逐渐获得这方面知识的，这给我带来了非常痛苦的打击，我因此受到很大的触动。

因为我得了一场大病，或者说得了好几种疾病，我几乎没能完成在实科中学的学业。我的病情岌岌可危，甚至医生都对我的康复不抱有任何希望，准备放弃治疗。患病期间，父亲允许我随意进行阅读，我从公众图书馆里面借阅了很多书籍，这家图书馆经常被人忽视，但是馆里的工作人员非常信任我，于是我得以参与图书的分类和编目工作。一天，馆里的人员带给我几本文学书籍，这是以前我没有阅读过的书籍，我很快沉迷于阅读的快乐之中，并使我彻底忘却了自身的病态。这几本书都是马克·吐温早期的小说，在阅读的过程中，我的身体竟然不可思议地好转起来。25年之后,我遇到了马克·吐温,我们很快结下了深厚的友谊,我把这段经历讲给他听,并惊奇地发现他笑出了眼泪。

后来,我升入了位于克罗地亚的卡尔斯塔德市的实科高中里继续学习,我的一个姑姑居住在那所城市。她本人很优秀,她的丈夫是陆军上校,参加过多次战斗,是一名久经沙场的骑兵战士。我在姑姑家里居住了3年,这段时光令我永生难忘。她家纪律严明,甚至比战争年代的堡垒还要严格。我就像金丝雀一样被喂养,所有的食物都是高品质的,制作精美,但是数量少得可怜,简直就是正常人的千分之一。我姑姑切出来的火腿片就像一张透明的纸张那样薄,即便如此,还是严格限制我的饮食。上校有时要给我多加一点菜肴,她都会拿走,并且会很激动地说道:"小心一点,尼克很精致,他吃不了那么多。"其实我胃口很好,但是却被迫承受坦塔罗斯一般的痛苦。

值得庆幸的是,除此之外,我生活的环境充满着优雅和艺术的气息,这在当时是非常特别的。这里地势低洼,沼泽众多,疟疾肆虐,虽然我服用了大量的奎宁,但仍然经常发烧。有时候,河水上涨,大量的老鼠涌入居民的家中,它们什么都啃,什么都吃,包括那些特别辛辣的红辣椒。这些害虫对于我来说,是一个很有意思的消遣。我采用各种手段对付它们,并且取得了胜利,为此我还在当地社区赢得了一个并不那么令人羡慕的称号——捕鼠者。最后，我完成了学业，痛苦随之结束。得到了毕业证书之后，我面临着命运的抉择。

那些年，我的父母一直想让我从事神职工作，其想法从来没有改变过，这一点让我感到非常的恐惧和害怕。我对电学一直抱有浓厚的兴趣，这主要是受到物理学教授的刺激性影响，他是一位天才型的人物，经常通过自己发明的装置来证明某些原理。在教授发明的这些装置中，我能够回忆起来的是一个能够自由旋转的灯泡形状的装置，锡箔涂层，当被连接到静电机器的时候，能够快速旋转。对我来说，我很难完全表述出自己面对这些现象时候所受到的强烈震撼。每次展示都会在我的脑海中激发上千次的共鸣，我想深入了解这种神奇的力量。我渴望投身于类似的实验和调查，但是现实让人痛苦，我可能被迫放弃这样的想法。

当我正准备返回家乡的时候，父亲却通过别人告诉我，他希望我去参加一个狩猎远征。这是一个奇怪的请求，因为他一直对这种运动嗤之以鼻。几天后，我知道家乡发生了霍乱，但是我仍然不顾父母的反对，返回了戈斯皮奇。这个地区每隔15年到20年就会爆发一次霍乱，人们对于引发它的原因却一无所知，这一点令人难以置信。他们把原因归结于空气中刺鼻的味道和烟雾。与此同时，却一直在饮用那些被污染的不洁水源，这导致人员大批死亡。我也身患疾病，在床上恐惧地躺了整整9个月的时间不能移动。我的精力已经全部耗尽，第二次我发现我来到了死亡的边缘。

我的生命危在旦夕，正在这时，我的父亲冲进了我的房间，他的脸色苍白，但是仍然在安慰我，试图让我看到他脸上的自信。我说道："如果你让我学习工程学，也许我会康复的。"于是他郑重承诺："你将进入世界上最好的工程学院。"我相信父亲的承诺，心里的一块石头落下了，但是这还要感恩一种治疗方法，我喝了一种奇怪的豆子熬制的汤，并且因此得以康复，如果没有身体的康复，一切都毫无意义。我神奇般的康复经历，就如同拉撒路的复活一样，每个人对此都感到非常震惊。

我的父亲坚持让我花费一年的时间进行户外运动，以保持身体的健康，我非常不愿意这样做，但是别无选择。于是，在这一学年的大部分时间里，我携带着猎人的装备和很多书籍，在山里漫游，与自然的亲密接触使我的身体与思想变得一样健康。我不断地进行思索和规划，萌发出了很多构想，但是却缺乏对于原理的掌握。图像非常清晰，但是知识却非常有限。在其中的一个构想之中，我设想通过海洋传递信件和包裹，具体方法是在海底搭建一个管道，但是要有足够的强度来抵制液压。我设想了一个抽水的装置，能够给水施加压力流过管道，所有的细节都考虑在内，但是有一个问题被我忽视掉了。我认为水的速度比较随意，而且可以任意提高水速，从而通过毫无缺陷的运算达到完美的效果。但是，随后证明，管道对于水流产生的阻力是个问题，我无能为力，只能把这个想法公开，看看其他人能否做到这一点。

我的另外一个构想，就是围绕赤道打造一个圆环，它可以自由浮动，也可以在旋转的过程中被反作用力所控制，这样人们旅行的速度就可以达到每小时1 000千米，这在铁路运行中是完全不可能达到的高速度。看到这个想法，读者们一定会觉得非常可笑，因为这项计划几乎不具备可操作性。我承认这一点，但是其实还存在比我更为异想天开的人，纽约有一位非常著名的教授，曾经设想把热带的空气抽送到温带，他完全忽略了这样一个事实，上帝为实现这个目的已经制造出一台巨大的机器。

还有一个更重要、更有吸引力的方案是从地球的旋转中获得能量。我发现了这样一个事实，由于地球的昼夜转动，地球表面物体的运动方向，有时候与平移的运动同向，有时候则是反方向。从这个结果来看，可以通过最简单的方式利用巨大的能量，从而为地球上任何宜居的地区提供动能。但是后来我异常沮丧，甚至无法用语言描述出那种失望之情，我陷入了和阿基米德一样的困境，就像他一直在徒劳地寻找宇宙的支点。

休假和调养结束之后，我被送到了施第里尔格拉茨的一所理工学院，这是父亲为我选择的学校，它是最古老、最有名望的研究机构之一。这是我梦寐以求的机遇，我满腔热情地投入了学业之中，并下定决心一定要走向成功。我以前的学术训练要高于一般水平，主要原因在于父亲的教导和提供的机会。我精通几门语言，浏览了很多图书馆的藏书，得到了或多或少有用的信息。而且，在大学，我可以第一次自主选择喜欢的科目，甚至连徒手绘画对于我来说都不再是一种困扰了。

我下定决心，要取得好成绩，要给父母以惊喜。在整个第一学年里，我一般都是凌晨3点起床开始学习，一直到晚上11点，周末和节假日也不例外。我的大部分同学都满足于取得及格的成绩，但是我的目标更为远大，我要刷新成绩的记录单。第一学年，我一共考了9门课，教授们认为满分已经不能很好地界定我的学业。我带着这些傲人的成绩，回到家乡，短暂休息，期待家人的表扬，然而父亲对于我取得的成绩似乎不屑一顾，我深受打击。但是在他去世之后，我发现了一捆信件，是教授们写给他的，他们担心我过于拼命的后果，认为如果父亲继续让我在学校学习，我可能会过劳而死。

此后，我主要从事物理、力学和数学研究，业余时间主要在图书馆里看书。无论做任何事情，我都力求速度，追求尽善尽美，这经常使我陷入困境。有一次，我开始阅读伏尔泰的作品，令我苦恼不堪的是，他的著作有100卷，而且全部是小字体印刷，这个怪才为了完成这些著作，每天都要喝72杯黑咖啡。最终，我阅读了他的全部著作，当我看完最后一本的时候，我非常喜悦，同时也暗下决心："以后再也不能这么阅读了"。

我在第一学年的表现异常出色，也因此赢得了几位教授的欣赏，并和他们建立起了深厚的友谊，包括：罗格纳教授，他教授数学和几何；波什尔教授，是理论和实验物理实验室的主任；阿莱博士，讲授积分学，特别擅长微分方程。阿莱博士是我听过的讲座之中最具智慧的演说家。他对我的进步非常关注，经常在教室里面多待上一两个小时，给我提出问题，让我来解决，我也乐此不疲。我向他谈到了我构想过的飞行器，那不是一种虚幻的发明，而是基于声音和科学原理的构想，通过涡轮机，它是可以实现的，而且很快将会出现在世人面前。罗格纳教授和波什尔教授都是好奇心很重的人。前者展现自己的方式非常特别，在表达问题的时候，总是有一段很长的、甚至令人感到尴尬的停顿。波什尔教授是一位很有条理的、非常理性的德国人。他的四肢都很庞大，就像熊爪一样，但是他做实验非常精确，就像时钟一样，没有丝毫的误差。

在第二学年，我们收到了一台来自巴黎的格拉姆发电机，它的配置包括马蹄形状的薄片磁铁，还有金属丝缠绕的带有整流器的电枢。一旦连接起来，就会展现出各种电流的效果。当波什尔教授进行展示的时候，他把这台机器作为电动机进行操作，结果刷子出现了故障，到处都是火花，我观察后得出结论，如果没有这些装备，也可以对电动机进行操作。波什尔教授指出，这似乎不大可能，但他给了我一个机会，让我在课堂上讲述我的观点。他的评论是："特斯拉先生是能够成就伟业的人，但是在这件事情上不会成功。这就如同把一个诸如地心引力的恒定拉力，转换成为一种旋转的力量。这是一个永动的构想，是不可能实现的幻想。"但是，直觉有时真的能够超越常识。毫无疑问，我们拥有更好的神经纤维，能够在推理或者其他的努力无法达成目标的前提下发现真理。因为教授的权威论断，我一度动摇过，但是很快我又坚定了自己的决心，以青春的激情和无限的信心投入了研究之中。

我在脑海里面构建了一个直流电动机，并且在头脑中运行它，跟踪电枢中的电流变化。随后，我又想象出一个交流发电机，并且以同样的方式运行了整个过程。接下来，我又设想了机器的构成，包括发动机和发电机，用不同的方式对它们进行操作。我看到的图片都是极为真实的，就像触手可及一样。在格拉茨其余的学期里面，我一直都非常努力，但是徒劳无功，就和这次一样，最后，我也认为，问题可能真的是没有办法解决了。

1880年，我来到了波西米亚的布拉格，这也是为了实现父亲的愿望，要在那里完成我的大学学业。正是在布拉格，我获得了关键的进展，把整流器从机器上剥离下来，从这个新的角度去研究问题，但是仍然没有取得实效。第二年，我的生活理念突然发生了重大变化。我意识到，为了我的成长，父母已经付出了很多，于是决心参加工作减轻他们的负担。那时，从美国兴起的电话浪潮开始波及欧洲大陆，大陆上开始设立电话局，其中有一个就设置在匈牙利的布达佩斯。这是一个理想的机遇，而且，我们家族的一个朋友正好是企业的负责人，但却是在这里，我的精神突然彻底崩溃，就和以前经历过的一样。

在这期间，我所经历的一切，超越了所有人的想象。我的视觉和听力一直特别突出。我能够非常清晰地辨别出远方的物体，而其他人甚至连影子都没有看到。还有几次，我为邻居的房子预报了火情，因为我听到了非常微弱的噼啪的声音，那时声音还非常弱小，睡眠中的邻居完全没有意识到这些，我听到后及时叫醒了他们，预防了火灾的发生。

1899年，我刚刚过完40岁的生日，在科罗拉多做实验，当时我能够在550英里[①]之外听到打雷的声音。而我年轻的助手听力的范围不超过150英里。我的耳朵灵敏度是常人的13倍。但是此时，与我神经高度紧张时期敏锐的听力相比，我的听觉几乎是完全丧失的状态。在布达佩斯的时候，我能够听到隔着三个房间的钟表的滴答声音。一只苍蝇萦绕在房间里面的桌子上，就会在我的耳朵里引发一声闷响。几英里之外行驶的马车，也会引发我身体的激烈反映。二三十英里之外的机车声音，也会导致我感觉到自己坐的椅子在激烈震动，引发我无尽的痛苦。由于机车来来往往，我脚下的地面一直处于震动之中，我只有在床底下垫上橡胶垫子，这样我才能够适当休息。来自远远近近的喧闹声音，其效果就像有人在我耳边喃喃低语，如果不能辨别出来，我就会感到非常害怕。当阳光断断续续地照射进来的时候，就会作用于我的脑海，令我感到眩晕不已。当我走过桥梁或者其他类似结构的建

---

① 1英里＝1.609 344千米。

筑物的时候，我必须调动全身的力量，因为我的头骨会感受到超强的压力。在黑暗来临的时候，我感觉自己就像一只蝙蝠，能够感受到距离我12英尺①以外物体的存在，前额的地方有一种特别恐怖的感觉。我的脉搏变化多端，有时只有几次，有时会达到260次，似乎身体所有的器官都在颤抖，这是最令人难以忍受的事情，一位非常著名的内科医生，建议我每天服用大量的溴化钾，他说我的病是极为罕见的，根本无法治愈。

我最大的遗憾是，我的经历如此独特，却没有生理学家和心理学家对此进行跟踪监测。为了生存，我苦苦挣扎，从来没有想过自己会康复。有谁会相信，一个毫无希望的病弱之躯竟然发生了惊人的转变，充满了力量，充满了韧性，工作了长达38年的时间，几乎没有一天休息的时间，而且不知疲倦，仍然身体强壮，思维敏锐？这就是我的真实经历。强烈的生存愿望，继续工作的热情，以及一位极其忠诚的朋友的帮助，所有这些因素共同创造出了奇迹。我的健康回归了，同时又充满了思维的活力，精神焕发。在问题得到解决的时候，我有时甚至感到遗憾，这场战斗结束得过于仓促，我还有很多过剩的精力。当我开始接手这项任务

---

① 1英尺＝0.304 8米。

的时候，并没有像其他人那样痛下决心。对于我来说，这是神圣的誓言，事关生死。如果我失败了，我只能走向灭亡。现在，我赢得了战斗。解决方法在于大脑深处，但是我还不能把它表述出来。在我的回忆里，某一天下午，我和一位朋友在城市公园里散步，边走边朗诵诗歌。当时，我能够一字不差记下整本书。其中有一首就是歌德的《浮士德》，当时正是日落时分，于是我想到了其中的某些段落：

> 夕阳西下，白昼宣告了它的结束；
> 乌鸦飞走了，兔子也不见了；
> 新的生活开始了；
> 可惜我不曾拥有翅膀，
> 不能追逐太阳！
> 这一切只是我的美丽幻想，
> 太阳已经落山，
> 哎，肉体的翅膀，
> 无论如何，都无法与精神的翅膀相媲美！

当我说出这些鼓舞人心的诗句之时，就像一道闪电击中了我的大脑，然后就突然发现了真理。我随后用一根棍子在沙地上画出了我的想法，6年之后，我在美国电器工程师协会之前展示了我的成果，我散步时候的同伴非常了解这一点。我所看到的图像非常清晰，具有金属和石头般的坚固性，于是我告诉他："看啊，这里是我的发动机，看我如何翻转它。"我无法描述出自己的感觉。我的感觉就如同皮格马利翁看到自己的雕塑作品复活一般。我可能在无意之中发现了1 000个大自然的机密，即便如此，我也会用它们换取这样的发现，为了它，我曾经排除万难，甚至挣扎在生存的边缘。

第四章 特斯拉线圈和变压器的发现

在某个时期，我完全沉浸在对于机械进行绘制和设计之中，这是一种极致的享受，也是在我的有生之年，充分体会到完整幸福的一段时期。思维的火花源源不断地浮现于我的脑海之中，我面临的唯一挑战就是需要尽快地捕捉它们。对于我而言，我所构想的装置的每一个细节，都是绝对真实的存在，几乎达到了触手可及的程度，甚至时间标志和磨损的标志都能够分辨出来。我的眼前浮现出这样一幅画面，马达在永不停歇地运转，从而呈现出一道极为迷人的风景。当孕育在内心的兴趣，最终发展成为一种强烈的愿望，当工作成为一种爱好，一个人奔向目标的速度就会大大加快，就如同穿上了童话中的七里格鞋子一样。在不到两个月的时间里，我几乎研究了所有类型的马达，对其系统进行了修改，现在它们都以我的名字进行了命名。但是，这种研究实在耗费脑力，可能比较幸运的是，我的活动突然面临暂停。

我来到了布达佩斯，这主要是受一份特别不成熟的关于电话行业的报告的影响。或许，这也是命运的嘲讽，我不得不在匈牙利中央电报办公室接受一个绘图员的职位。至于薪水问题，因为这是政府的秘密，我也避而不谈吧。很幸运的是，总督察非常欣赏我，于是我被任命负责所有与新设备有关的运算、设计和评估方面的工作，一直到电话开始正常运营，随后我仍然负责这些工作。在这一过程中，我获得了多方面的知识和丰富的工作经验，这些都是极为宝贵的经历，也使得我发明的设备得到了运用和检验的机会。我改进了中央电报工作室的一些设备，完善了一种电话中继器或放大器，它从未获得专利，我也没有在公开场合说起

特斯拉与特斯拉线圈

过它，但直至今日，我也相信这是值得称颂的行为。为了回报我卓有成效的协助行为，也是出于对我个人贡献的肯定，企业的主管人士普斯卡斯先生，在转让了布达佩斯的生意之后，给我提供了一个在巴黎的工作岗位，我愉快地接受了。

巴黎是一座神奇的城市，给我留下了深刻的印象，令我难以忘怀。在我抵达巴黎之后的头几天，我一直在街道上漫步，陶醉于其新奇的景观。巴黎吸引人的地方很多，魅力十足，令人难以抗拒，但可惜的是，我的工资很快就花光了。当普斯卡斯先生问我是否适应新环境的时候，我对自己情形的描述就是："每个月最后的29天，都是最为艰难的时光"。在巴黎，我过着一种几乎苦行僧般的生活，现在的人们称之为"罗斯福式的时尚"。不论天气如何变幻，每天早晨我都会从自己居住的圣马赛尔大道出发，来到塞纳河畔的一所游泳馆，在水里遨游27个来回，然后我会步行一个小时，来到伊夫里，那是公司工厂所在的地方。7点半，我与伐木工人一起吃早餐，然后就会等待午餐时光的来临。上午，我会为经理查尔斯·巴切尔（Charles Batchellor）先生处理非常棘手的问题，他是爱迪生先生的密友和助手。

在这里，我接触到几位美国人，因为我擅长打台球，他们特别喜欢和我在一起玩。我给他们解释了自己的发明，其中一位是美国人，即机械部门的领班坎宁安先生，给我提出了建议，要我组建一个股份公司。当时我认为这个建议简直滑稽至极。我只知道，这是美国人的行为方式，但是对于股份公司毫无概念。于是，这个建议石沉大海，在接下来的几个月里面，为了解决发电厂出现的各种问题，我奔波于法国和德国的多个城市之间。最终回到巴黎之后，我向公司的一位行政主管劳先生提出了一个建议，要求改进发电机，他同意给我一个机会。我取得了完全的成功，董事们欣喜异常，于是给了我发展自动稳压器的特权，这是我一直以来非常渴望的发明。不久，在阿尔萨斯斯特拉斯堡新建成的火车站的照明设备出现了问题，其布线存在问题，在德国皇帝威廉一世出席的开幕式上，由于电线短路发生了爆炸，很大一部分的墙面被炸毁了。德国政府拒绝接收这样的火车站，法国的公司面临困境，可能遭遇巨大损失。考虑到我会德语，以及过去的出色经历，我被派去解决这个难题，于是1883年年初，我临危受命，前往斯特拉斯堡。

  那个城市发生的一些事件令我印象深刻，甚至可以说是刻骨铭心。很有意思的是，有一种很奇怪的巧合，那个城市在那个时期出现了不少名人。后来，我这样说道："这座城市有一种被称为'伟大'的细菌，其他人被感染了，但是我却逃开了。"在那里，我非常忙碌，不分昼夜地处理出现的各种问题，与法国公司保持通信联系，与当地的官员开会，但是我很快就理顺了这一切。我在火车站对面的机械商店里面，组建出一台非常简单的发电机，当时我从巴黎带来了一些材料。但是，这个实验的进程不断被耽搁，直到夏天，我才算取得了比较满意的成果。通过转变不同相位的交流电，即便没有转向器或者滑动接触器，电机也可以正常运转，这与我一年之前的构想完全符合。这种快乐的感觉非常美妙，随后的第一次展示给我带来了更为狂热的快乐感觉。

在我新结交的朋友之中，有一位是这座城市的前任市长鲍津先生（Mr. Bauzin），他已经熟悉了我的各种发明。我努力争取他的支持。他也在竭尽所能地帮助我，把我的发明推荐给了几个富有的人，但是令我感到屈辱的是，我没有得到任何回应。他尝试通过各种办法来帮助我，其中1919年7月1日那一天令我终生难忘，这件事情一直在提醒我，一定要牢记所得到的帮助，心存感恩之心。虽然他没有直接给我金钱上的资助，但他的帮助却具有同等的价值。1870年，当德国人侵入这个国家的时候，鲍津先生把一批非常好的1801年生产的圣埃斯蒂菲酒掩埋起来，他认为除了我之外，没有人有资格享受这种昂贵的酒品。这可以说是我一生中最难忘的事情之一。我的这位朋友力主我返回巴黎，在那里寻求赞助。我也迫切希望返回巴黎，但是因为各种各样的琐碎小事，我的工作和谈判不断推迟，我的处境看起来让人感到绝望。

为了让大家了解一下德国人的严肃认真、一丝不苟和极高的"效率"，我给大家讲一件我经历过的有趣的事情。我们当时计划在走廊上安装一盏16功率的白炽灯，选好位置之后，我让装配工去布线。操作了一会儿之后，这位工人认为必须咨询工程师才能继续进行操作。后者提出了一些不同意见，最终同意灯泡应该安装在距离我原来设计地点2英寸的地方，于是布线工作得以继续。随后，工程师又开始忧心忡忡，告诉我这件事情应该向检查员埃维戴克请示。于是，这位重要的人物不断打电话、调查和讨论，最后决定这盏灯应该后退2英寸，这也是我曾经标记过的地方。但是，不久，埃维戴克又临阵退缩，告诉我他已经通知了工程的督察希罗尼穆斯，我应该等待他的抉择。这位督察工作繁忙，几天之后才从其他事务中得以脱身，最后他来到现场，经过两个小时的讨论，我决定把安装的位置再向前移动2英寸。我真的希望这是最后的决定，再也不想被这个问题所困扰了。结果，这位总督察再度返回，对我说道："冯克是一个很特别的人，在没有得到他的明确批示之前，我不能决定这盏灯应该放在哪里。"于是，我们又开始预约这位重要人物的来访，为此进行准备。我们很早就起来打扫卫生，进行清扫工作。每个人都要做好准备，我戴上了手套，当冯克及随从到来的时候，他受到了隆重的接待。经过两个小时的协商之后，他突然说"我得走了"，然后指向天花板上的某个位置，让我把白炽灯安装在那里。这其实就是我最初选择的地方。

日复一日，变化不断地发生，但是我决心无论付出何种代价，都要实现自己的目标，我的努力最终得到了回报。到了1884年春天，所有的分歧都被调整过来，工程最终被接受，我回到了巴黎，心中充满期待，因为我们的主管之一曾经向我承诺，如果这件事情取得圆满成功，我将得到慷慨的奖赏，因为我在发动机上所做的改进，我觉得这比较公平，我应该得到物质上的补偿。公司有3名管理人员，为了简明起见，我分别称他们为A、B和C。我拜访了A，他告诉我自己无法决定，B拥有发言权。但是B先生认为他同样没有发言权，只有C才有决定权，而C肯定地告诉我，A拥有最终决定权。经过几次的这种推诿，我突然意识到所谓的奖赏就是空中楼阁，就如同西班牙的城堡一样遥不可及。

我遭遇到的另一个打击，就是试图为我的进一步发展筹集资金，最终也以失败告终。我感到灰心丧气，正在此时，巴切勒先生劝说我去往美国，他认为我对爱迪生机器的重新设计就是最好的敲门砖，我心动了，决心去往这块黄金之地试试运气。于是我带着自己非常有限的财产，准备乘坐火车，但是当火车已经驶出的时候，我发现自己仍然滞留在火车站里面，因为那时我发现自己的钱包和车票都不见了。我该怎么办？大力神有足够的时间加以考虑，但是我必须立即做出决定，两种对立的念头一直在我的脑海里斗争，就像冷凝器在震动一样。最后，我及时做出了决定，就像忘却不愉快的小事一样，我决定带着剩余的东西乘船奔向纽约，包括我写的诗歌和一些文章，还有一些关于积分和飞行器的未解难题。在海上旅程中，我经常坐在船尾，希望遇到一个机会把某人从水里解救出来，一点儿都没有考虑到危险性的问题。后来，我接受了一些美国的实用主义观念，我对这种想法感到不可思议，并且为自己的愚蠢感到惊讶不已。

我一直希望能够说出自己对这个国家的第一印象。在我读过的阿拉伯故事里面，魔仆把人们运送到能够美梦成真的地方，通过愉快的冒险，人们最终实现了自己的愿望，但是我的经历正好相反。魔仆把我从一个梦想的世界带到了一个现实的世界。我离开的地方是美丽的、充满艺术气息的，在各个层面都充满迷人的魅力；但是我在这里看到的是机器化的、粗糙的、毫无吸引力的地方。一个身材魁梧的警察正在摆弄警棍，在我看来，这根警棍就如同一根圆木那么粗大。我非常礼貌地向他询问道路,"向下走6个街区,然后左拐。"他回答说,目光如炬。"这难道就是美国吗?"我痛苦地问自己,"这是一个在文明上落后于西方的国家。"但是后来我的想法发生了转变,当我在1889年离开美国的时候——那也是我抵达美国5年之后,我开始意识到美国要领先于欧洲100多年,时至今日,我的这种想法再也没有发生过动摇。

与爱迪生的会晤是我终生难忘的事件之一。我对这个杰出的男人充满好奇之心,他不是天才,也没有受过科学的训练,但是却取得了很大的成功。我学了12门语言,钻研文学和艺术,把我最好的时光献给了图书馆,阅读了各种各样的书籍,从牛顿的《原理》到保罗·德·科克的小说,都在我的阅读范围之内,感觉自己浪费了人生的大部分时光。但是不久,我就意识到这是我一生中做过的最值得的事情。仅仅几个星期之后,我就赢得了爱迪生的信任,具体经过是这样的。当时速度最快的客轮名为"S.S.俄勒冈号",它有两套照明设备,全部出现了故障,于是其行程被耽搁了。因为客轮的上部是在照明设备安装好之后才建造起来的,所以不可能把它们挪开进行修理。问题很严重,爱迪生深受其扰。晚上的时候,我带着各种工具,登上了船只,在船上工作了一整夜。发电机的情况非常糟糕，有几处出现了短路，在船员的帮助下，我成功解决了故障。第二天早晨5点，当我沿着第五大道走向办公地点的时候，我遇到了爱迪生、巴彻勒和其他几个人，他们正准备回家休息，爱迪生说道："看我们的巴黎人，整晚都不知道跑到哪里去了。"我告诉他，我刚从俄勒冈号回来，把两套设备都修复了。他看着我，一言未发，然后走开了。走了一段距离之后，我听到了他的评价："巴彻勒真是一个好人啊。"从那之后，我有了开展工作的完全自由。

在长达一年的时间里，我的工作时间是从上午10点30分到第二天凌晨5点，全年无休。爱迪生跟我说："我有很多工作努力的助手，但你的确是最优秀的。"在这期间，我设计了24种不同的标准机器，用非常短的磁芯和统一的模式取代了旧的部件。经理答应我，如果我完成任务，就会给我5万美金，但结果却是一场恶作剧。这种打击让我极度痛苦，于是我辞职了。

不久，就有人找到我，提出以我的名义建立弧光公司，我答应了。我认为这给我提供了一个研究发动机的机会，但是当我向我的合作者提出研制方案的时候，他们的回答是："不，我们只需要弧光灯，我们对你的交流电毫无兴趣。"1886年，我的弧光照明系统取得了完美成功，工厂和公用场所的照明都采用了这一技术，我自由了，但是除了一张非常漂亮的只具有想象价值的股权证书，我再没有得到其他的任何东西。随后我经历了一段在新领域奋斗的时光，我并不擅长于此，但是最终得到了回报，1887年4月，我组建了特斯拉电器公司，提供了一个实验室和相关设备，我在那里构建了发电机，它和我想象得完全一致。我没有追求任何的改善，仅仅提供了我脑海中浮现的图纸，操作情况也和我想象的完全一致。

1888年早期，我与西屋电器公司打成了协议，开始大规模生产发电机。这的确需要克服很多的困难，我的系统设计是基于低频率的电流，而西屋公司的专家采用的是133周期的方案，其目标是寻求转换方面的优势。他们不想脱离他们设备的标准形式，于是我不得不对发电机进行改造，以适应他们的需求。另外，我还需要做的工作就是生产出一种发电机，能够以这样的频率在两根电线上运转，这的确不大容易成功。

在1889年即将结束的时候，我在匹兹堡的工作基本完成，返回了纽约，在格朗街的一个实验室里继续进行实验工作，在那里，我全身心地投入高频率机器的设计中去。这个问题没有人涉猎过，是新奇的、特别的，我遇到了很多困难。我拒绝采用感应发电器的模式，担心它可能不会产生完美的正弦波，这对共振的行动是非常重要的。要不是出于这个目的,我本来是可以省心省力的。高频交流发电机的另一个令人感到沮丧的缺点似乎是速度的不稳定性,这严重限制了它的使用。在美国电气工程师协会的几次展示中,我已经好几次观察到调谐出现了问题,需要进行重新调整,但是我当时并没有预见性,很久之后我才发现了一种操纵机器的手段,也就是速度在两个极端的负荷之间不能变化太快。

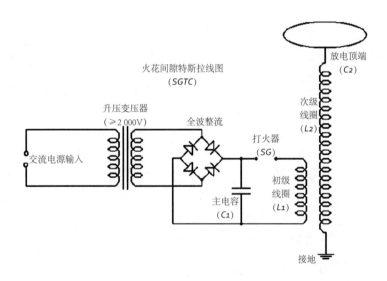

特斯拉线圈的原理图

由于多种因素的影响，设计一种更简单的装置来产生电流震动似乎是很必要的。1856年，开尔文男爵提出了电容放电的理论，但是没有被应用到实际操作中去。我看到了该理论应用的实际可能性，开始应用这一原理进行感应设置的开发。我的进展非常顺利，所以在1891年发表演讲的时候，能够展示一个释放出5英寸火花的线圈。在演讲的场所，我非常坦率地告诉在座的各位工程师，在用新方法进行转化的时候，存在一个缺陷，就是火花间隙会造成损失。随后的研究显示，任何介质的采用，包括空气、氢、水银蒸气、油或者电子流，效率都是相同的。这是一种非常类似于控制机械转换能量的定律。我们可以从一个高度垂直向下抛掷一个具有一定重量的物体，或者把它带到较低的地方，让它曲线前进，这看起来在消耗上没有什么区别。幸运的是，这个缺点并不致命，只要共振电路比例恰当，就能够达到85%的效率。自从这项早期的发明宣布以来，它已经被广泛采用，给很多领域带来了革命性的变化。而且，这一发明还有很多光辉的前景。1900年，我收获到了100英尺的强力放电，并在世界范围内引发了闪电效应。这一景象让我想起了我在格朗街实验室观察到的第一个火花，那是一种非常激动人心的感觉，就如同我发现旋转磁场的时候一样。

第五章 不断放大的发射机的发明

当我回顾以往生活和工作经历的时候,才开始意识到塑造我们命运的力量极其微妙。我年轻时经历的一个偶然事件可以解释这一现象。一个冬日,我和几个伙伴计划一起攀爬一座陡峭的山坡。雪很厚,空中刮着南风,这是一个宜于爬山的天气。我们决定玩滚雪球的游戏,我们各自滚出一个小雪球,然后沿着一定的距离滚下去,这个过程中雪球会或多或少地粘上一些雪,从而有所增大。我们都试图让自己的雪球更大,战胜别人,这个游戏很有趣,也非常激动人心。突然,一个雪球变得越来越大,变得像房子那么庞大,超出了它能够承受的极限,随后它滚进了山谷,发出"砰"的一声,地面随之颤抖起来。我茫然地看着这一切,完全无法理解所发生的事情。随后的几个星期,雪崩的画面不断浮现在我的面前,我一直很困惑,为什么那么小的东西会膨胀到那么大的体积。从那以后,我一直好奇于微弱的力量是如何放大的。几年之后,我对机械和电气共振进行了实验,这是我最初就充满兴趣的领域。但是,如果没有早期经历留下的深刻印象,那么我就不会执着于早期线圈上的小火花,也不会有后来的发明,这是我第一次把真相告诉大家。

经常有人问我,我最喜欢哪一项发明。这取决于个人的看法。大部分的技术人员,在自己特殊的领域里非常能干,但是学究气息过浓,目光也非常短浅。他们认为除了感应发电机之外,我对世界几乎没有做出什么实质性的贡献,这是完全的曲解和偏见。我们不能依据即时的结果来判定新思想的价值。我的电力传输系统主要是在心理层面发生的,这也是一个长久寻求的解决工业问题的方案,必须克服相当大的阻力,也需要协调各方的利益,但是如同其他技术一样,商业的推广不能再耽误了。例如,可以把这种情形与我的涡轮机发明时候的状况进行对比。有人可能会想,这台发电机简单、美观,拥有很多特别理想的特征,应该马上被采用,但是它与我的涡轮机面临同样的命运。旋转场的预期效果并不是要作废现在的机器效能,相反,是要给它提供附加的价值。这个系统既有利于新企业,也有利于老企业的改善。我的涡轮机是全新的进步,它的采用与成功并不意味着原来价值几百亿美元的动力机的彻底废弃。在当时的情况下,进展必须非常缓慢，最大的阻力可能主要来自有组织的专家们头脑中所产生的偏见。

就在前几天，我遇到了我的朋友和前助理查尔斯·f.斯科特，他是耶鲁大学电气工程教授，这次会面让我非常沮丧。我已经很久没有看到他了，所以我很高兴有机会和他在办公室闲聊一会儿。我们很自然地谈到了我的涡轮机，于是谈话开始变得热烈起来。"斯科特，"我沉浸在未来的辉煌愿景之中，"我的涡轮机将使得世界上所有的热机都被废止。"斯科特抚摸着自己的下巴，边想边把眼光投向别的地方，好像在盘算着什么似的，然后说道："那将出现大量的废铁。"然后就一言不发地转身离开了。

但是，我的很多发明都只是在每个方向上前进了几小步而已。在这一过程中，我只是遵循自己的直觉对于现有的装置进行改进，没有任何功利性的特殊想法。"放大的发射机"是我数年以来持续不断工作的结果，最为主要的目标是为了解决人类面临的更为重要的问题，而不仅仅是出于工业发展的需要。

如果我的记忆比较准确的话，1890年11月，我在实验室做了一个很有趣的实验，《科学》年报曾经对此有过记载，认为这是最特别的实验之一。在研究高频电流的时候，我特别满意的一点就是，当一个空间的电场达到足够的强度时就可以完全照亮无电极的真空管。随后，我拿出一个变压器来测试该理论，第一次试验就取得了圆满的成功。我们当时很难理解这些奇怪的现象究竟意味着什么。我们一直渴望着新的感觉，但是很快就变得对它们漠不关心。昨天的奇迹，到今日可能就变得稀松平常。当我的真空管第一次被公开展示出来的时候，人们的惊讶之情无以言表。我收到了来自世界各地的紧急邀请函，获得了很多的荣誉，也受到了很多的奉承，但是我不为所动，拒绝了这些邀请和荣誉。

但是，在1892年，有个要求实在让人无法拒绝，于是我前往伦敦，为英国电器工程师协会做了一次演讲。我的计划是演讲结束马上离开，去往巴黎进行一次同样无法推却的演讲。但是詹姆斯·杜瓦爵士坚持要求我在英国皇家研究院再发表一次演讲。我其实是一个非常坚定自律的人，但是这位伟大的苏格兰人的话实在极具说服力，所以我最终答应了。他把我推到一把椅子上坐下，往杯子里面倒入了半杯褐色的、看起来非常神奇的饮料，饮料看起来闪闪发光，喝起来就如同花蜜一样可口。他说道："现在，你坐的椅子是法拉第曾经坐的椅子，你喝的这种饮料也是法拉第所喜欢的威士忌。"这两个方面的体验的确都是令人羡慕的经历。第二天晚上，我在皇家研究院做了展示，瑞利勋爵在结束的时候面对公众发表了评论性讲话，他的慷慨表扬给了我很大的鼓励，这是我事业中第一次面临这样的局面。回到家乡之后，我又经历了痛苦的折磨，身患疾病。康复之后，我开始制定在美国恢复工作的计划。一直到那时，我也没有意识到自己拥有发明创造的天赋，然而瑞利勋爵对此深信不疑，我一直认为他才是最适合从事科学研究的人，他认为我应该充分发挥自己的天资，把精力集中在最为重要的事务上面。

一天，我正在山里散步，突然天气突变，暴风雨即将来临，我到处寻找能够避雨的地方。天空中乌云密布，但是雨水却似乎被耽搁了，迟迟没有降落下来。突然，天空之中出现了一道闪电，很快，暴风雨降临了。这种景象令我浮想联翩。很明显，这两种现象之间关系密切，存在因果联系，这种微小的反应使我得出的结论是，降水过程中所蕴含的电能是无法估量的，闪电的功能就像是一个敏感的触发器，能够把这种能量释放出来。

这种发现有可能产生极为惊人的成就。如果我们能够产生符合质量要求的电能效应，那么这个星球及其提供的生存条件都可以被扭转。阳光导致海洋的水面上升，风力则把它吹到遥远的地方，从而保持着最微妙的平衡状态。如果我们有能力在需要的时候破坏这种平衡，那么这个强大的维持生命的河流就会被控制住。我们可以灌溉干燥的沙漠，创造出新的湖泊和河流，并无限制地提供动力。这将是最有效的利用太阳能为人类提供服务的方式。这一完善依赖于我们在自然界中发展电力的能力。这似乎是无望之举，但我下定决心试一试，并立即返回美国。1892年的夏天，我开始了自己的工作，这个项目特别有吸引力，因为成功的话，我就可以利用它实现无线能量传播。

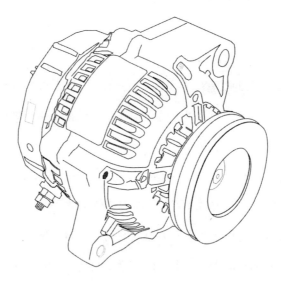

交流发电机

第二年的春天，我取得了第一项令人满意的成果。我通过自己的锥形线圈获得了大约1 000 000伏特的电压。按照现在的标准，这个数字不是很大，但在当时被视为一项壮举。我的实验一直在稳步前进，直到1895年我的实验室因为火灾被毁，马丁在《世纪杂志》四月份的刊号中发表了一篇文章，我们可以看到这场火灾的相关信息。这场灾难使我在很多方面的进展被迫倒退，那一年的大部分时间，我都埋头于进行规划和实验室的重建工作。但是只要条件允许，我马上又开始着手开展工作。

我也知道，使用更大规模的装置可以获得更高的电动力。但是，本能的直觉告诉我，一种规模相对较小而紧凑的变压器的设计，也可以实现同样的目标。在以平螺旋的形式进行实验的时候，就像我在专利中所解释的那样，电子束的缺失令我感到非常震惊，不久我就发现，这是因为线圈匝数的位置以及它们彼此之间的相互作用。得益于这种观察，我借助于使用更为高压的导体，其直径较大，能够保证间距，并且控制分散的能量，同时防止在任何一点上过度积累电荷。这种原理的运用使我能够获得4 000 000伏的电压，这是我在豪斯顿街的新实验室能够获得的最大极限值，因为这种放电能够延伸的距离是16英尺。这一发射器的照片刊登在1898年11月的《电气评论》杂志上。

为了沿着这条路径继续走下去，我必须进入更为开阔的空间，1899年春天，我已经完成了建设无线电站的准备工作，我去了科罗拉多，在那里居住了一年多的时间。在那里，我引进了其他的改进和完善措施，从而能够产生出所需要的各种强度的电流。那些对此感兴趣的人，可以在我的文章《关于人类能量不断增长的问题》找到一些在那里进行实验的相关信息，该篇论文发表于1900年6月的《世纪杂志》上面，我曾经在前面提到过这本杂志。

《电气实验》曾经要求我对这个课题做一简明的叙述，以便该杂志读者中的年轻人能够非常清晰地理解我的"放大发射机"的构造和操作情况，并进一步理解其目的所在。那么，好吧，我就进行一下介绍。首先，它是一个谐振变压器，每一部分都有次级电路，能够充电达到高电位，具有相当大的面积，在足够大的曲率半径之内沿着理想的包络面分布，彼此之间距离适当，从而保证到处都有很小的电流表面密度的存在，这样就不会出现漏电的现象，即使导体完全裸露在外，也不会漏电。它适合于任何频率，从每秒钟几个到上万个的周期都完全可以使用，因此可以用于生产流量巨大、中等压力的电流，也可以用于生产安培数较小、电动势能较大的电流。电压的大小仅仅是依赖于充电元件所在表面的曲率，以及元件的面积大小。

从我过去的经验来看，高达100 000 000伏特是完全可行的。另一方面，通过天线，就可以获得成千上万安培的电流。为了实现这样的操作，需要一个适当尺寸的装置。从理论上讲，一个直径小于90英尺的终端足以发展出这样大小的电动势，而天线的电流在通常的频率、直径不超过30英尺的条件下，就可以产生出2 000～4 000安培的电流。

如果进行更严格的限定，这种无线的发射器是一种赫兹波辐射，与整个能量相比，是一个完全可以忽略的量。在这种情况下，阻尼因子是极小的，而一个巨大的电荷储存在高容量中。这样的电路可能会被任何种类的脉冲所激发，即使是低频率的脉冲也能做到这一点。它可能产生正弦和连续振荡，就如同交流发电机一样。

然而，以这个术语最狭隘的意义来说，它是一个谐振变压器，除了拥有这些品质外，它还能精确地适应地球及其常数和特性，通过设计，它在通过无线方式进行能量传输方面更加高效。于是，距离造成的障碍被彻底消除，在发射脉冲的强度上衰减现象也不再出现。很有可能出现的情况是，依据一项非常准确的数学定律，随着设备安装距离的增加，行动的强度也会进一步增强。

这项发明是我的"世界系统"无线传输的一个案例。我于1900年返回纽约之后，开始了对这一系统进行商业化运作的过程。至于进行商业运营的直接目的，在这一时期的一项技术声明里面基本上比较明晰地表达出来了，下面我引用一下：

"世界系统"是由最初的几个发现组合而成的，这些发现都是发明者经过漫长的实验过程而创造出来的，它不仅使任何一种信号、消息或字符能够瞬时和精确地无线传输到世界各地，而且还使现有的电报、电话和其他信号站之间的相互连接不会发生任何变化。例如，通过它的运作，这里的电话用户可以打电话给全球任何其他用户。一个不超过手表大小的很便宜的接收器，就可以使得用户在任何地方（海洋和陆地都是如此）能够听到演讲或者现场演奏的音乐。

这些例子仅仅是为了说明这一伟大科学进步所创造出来的多种可能性。它湮灭了距离，使得地球成为最完美的自然导体，人类的聪明才智已经为一根线缆找到了无数的用途。这一系统造就的长期后果就是，任何能够通过一根或者多个电线操作的设备装置（当然是在限定的距离之内）都可以被驱动起来，即使在没有人工导体的情况下，只要具有相同功能的设施和精确度就可以实现这一目标，而且只要处在地球的物理维度之内，几乎不会受到任何的限制。因此，在这种理想的传播方式得以开发利用的情况下，不仅仅是商业领域的开发利用问题，传统领域也会得到极大的扩展。

世界系统的开发利用建立在以下重大发明和发现的基础之上：

1."特斯拉变压器"，这个装置是在电子振动的生产过程中产生的，具有革命性的意义，就如同火药对于战争的意义一样重大。这种方式产生的电流比通常方式产生的电流要多出很多倍，产生的火花超过100英尺长，这就是该发明的优势所在。

2."放大发射机"，这是特斯拉最好的发明，是一种极为特殊的变压器，能够激发地球，能够传导电能，这种传输只能使用天文望远镜进行观测。通过使用这种神奇的装置，他已经设置了比闪电更强的电流运动，通过的电流足以点亮全世界200多盏白炽灯。

3."特斯拉无线系统"，这个系统包括了一系列改进后的发明，而且是能够在无线状态下传输电能的唯一手段，成本低廉。仔细的测试和检验，以及科罗拉多发明者建立的能够进行伟大活动的试验站，已经证明这个系统可以传递任何大小的能量，必要的话甚至可以穿越地球，而损耗不会超过百分之几。

4. "个性化的艺术"。特斯拉的这项发明对于原始"调谐"的意义，就如同美妙的语言对于模糊的表达一样。它使信号或信息的传输绝对保密，并且在主动和被动方面，即非干扰和不可干扰的方面都是绝对保密的。每一个信号都像是一个明确无误的个体，而且在没有任何相互干扰的情况下，同时运行的电台或仪器的数量是无限的。

5. "陆地驻波"。通俗地说，这一伟大的发现，意味着地球对于特定音高的电波变化产生反应，就像音叉对于特定声波产生的反应一样。这些特殊的电子震动，能够有力地震动地球，能够在商业和其他许多方面，产生多种用途。

第一个"世界系统"电站即将在9个月内投入运行使用。通过该电厂的运行，可以得到1 000万马力的功率，可以同时为很多的技术成果服务，而且不需要额外附加的费用。

其中，下面的技术可能被包括在内：

1. 世界各地现有的电报交易所、办公室之间的相互联系。

2. 建立一个秘密的和不可干扰的政府电报服务。

3. 所有现有电话交换机或办公室在全球的互联。

4. 通过电报和电话与新闻界建立联系，使得普遍性新闻得到更广泛的传播。

5. 为了私人目的，建立一个情报传输的"世界系统"。

6. 世界各地股票行情的相互联系和运作。

7. 建立音乐发行的"世界体系"。

8. 使用廉价的钟表进行普遍的时间登记，每一个小时都会如同天文时间一般精确，不需要特别的管理。

9. 打字或手写字符、字母、支票等的世界传输。

10. 建立一种通用的海洋服务，使所有船舶的航海家在不需要指南针的情况下也能实现完美的航行，确定船只的准确地点、时间和速度，以防止碰撞和灾难等。

11. 海洋和陆地上的世界印刷系统的建立。

12. 世界范围内的摄影图片、各种图纸或记录的复制及传送。

我还曾经建议，进行小规模的无线传输的演示，这足以令人信服。除此之外，我还提到了其他的、无可比拟的关于我的发现的非常重要的应用，这些将在将来的某一天公布。长岛上将建立一座发电站，塔高达到187英尺，有一个直径长达68英尺的终端。这些尺寸足以传递任何能量。最初只能提供200到300千瓦的能量，但以后会逐渐发展到几千马力[①]。发射机发射的是一种非常有特点的波，我发明了一种非常独特的运用电话的方法，能够控制各种能量。

  这座塔在两年前就被毁坏了，但我的项目仍在继续开发中，也将构建另一座经过改进的试验塔。在这里，我想澄清一个流言，有人传说这座塔被政府蓄意毁坏，主要是积极备战的需要，这样的说法会强化某些人头脑之中的偏见，他们不知道美国政府曾经在30年前授予我美国公民的荣誉，对此我一直保密，还有一些勋章、证书、金牌和其他获得的荣誉都被我放在旧箱子里面。如果这个流言成真，那我将获得一大笔补偿，因为建塔的投入很大。相反，保留该塔符合政府的利益，因为它会实现政府的某些目标——我们这里只要提及一个有价值的结果就可以——可以在世界范围内确定一艘潜艇的位置。我的发电厂、服务和所有的改进技术一直任凭政府随意使用，自从欧洲冲突爆发以来，我牺牲了自己的某些发明工作，全身心地投入航空导航、船舶推进和无线传输等相关的工作中来，因为它们对于国家的安全至关重要。那些见多识广的人知道我的想法使美国的工业发生了革命性的变

---

① 1马力≈735瓦。

化，我不知道在这方面有哪个发明家和我一样幸运，因为我改进过的设备被美国政府广泛使用。在这个问题上，我没有公开地表达自己的观点，因为在整个世界都陷入可怕困境的时候，在个人事务上停留似乎是不恰当的。

鉴于关于我的各种流言蜚语，我还要补充一点，据说皮尔庞特·摩根先生对我的发明完全没有商业的兴趣，但他却资助了很多其他的开拓者。然而，实际的情况是他给予了我慷慨的资助，我不应该对他提出更多的要求。他对我的成就有着最高的敬意，并向我证明了他完全相信我具备最终实现我所要做的事情的能力。我不愿意让一些心胸狭窄的人满足于挫败我。这些人对我而言就是一种肮脏疾病的微生物细菌。我的计划被自然规律所阻碍。它太超前了，世界并没有为此做好准备。但自然规则终将生效，我也将取得最终的成功。

第六章 遥控力学的艺术

在我投入研究的所有项目之中，从来没有一个像放大发射机一样需要投入巨大精力的项目，这一发明对于脑细胞的使用甚至达到了比较危险的程度。青春年少的时候，我把激情和活力都奉献给了旋转磁场的发现之中，虽然工作也极端辛苦，但是具有完全不同的特征，没有涉及敏锐而令人筋疲力尽的洞察力，而这在解决无线电科学方面的问题上是必须加以运用的能力。尽管在进行放大发射机发明的时候，我的身体耐力很好，神经却出现了问题，最终彻底崩溃，那时漫长而艰巨的任务已经即将完成。

毫无疑问，这是上天的安排，赋予我一个安全阀，否则我将会在后来付出更大的代价，我的职业生涯可能也会被过早终止，这个安全阀随着时间的推移不断完善，当我的力量趋于耗尽的时候，它就会发出警告。所以，只要这个安全阀在运作，我就会远离因为劳累过度而带来的危险，这曾经是对其他发明家的致命威胁。顺便说一句,我并不需要对于大多数人而言必不可少的假期。我就像那些黑人一样"能够迅速进入睡眠状态,而白人只会整天忧心忡忡,容易导致失眠"。

每次从我的领域概括出一种新的理论,我的身体就会一点点地积累有毒的物质,于是我会陷入一种昏昏欲睡的状态,大概会持续半个小时。一觉醒来之后,我就会产生一种感觉,手边的工作好像是很久以前发生的事情,如果我继续进行被打断的工作,就会在心理上觉得非常恶心。于是我不情愿地被迫转向进行其他的工作。随后,我会惊讶地发现思维再度清晰起来,我克服了之前遇到的各种障碍。几个星期之后,有时是几个月之后,我又重新燃起了对这个暂时被抛弃的发明的热情,并能够迅速找到以前困扰我问题的答案,而且几乎没有付出任何过多的努力。

在这方面,我将讲述一些极为特殊的经历,心理学专业的学生可能对此颇感兴趣。我曾经用我的发射机观测到出一种极为惊人的现象,并且正在努力确定它与通过地球传播的电流的真正联系。这项工作的完成,看起来毫无希望,在一年多的时间里面,我一直为此坚持不懈,但是没有取得任何进展。我对这项研究投入了全部的精力,忘记了其他所有的事情,甚至忽略了我的健康。最后,当我快要崩溃的时候,我的保护机制启动了,于是进入了睡眠状态。当我清醒过来、感觉恢复之后，我惊讶地意识到，我已经无法回想起生活中的任何场景，除了婴幼儿时期还存有的记忆，那也是我刚刚有记忆的时期。奇怪的是，这些景象呈现在我的眼前，极度清晰，使我彻底放松下来。很多个夜晚，在我进入梦乡之前，我都会想起这些，以前的景象都浮现出来。我母亲的形象一直是那个慢慢展开的景象中的主要人物，我也产生了非常强烈的想看到她的愿望。这种感觉越来越强烈，我甚至决定放弃自己的工作去看望母亲。但是，我发现自己很难脱离实验室，几个月过去了，我已经把我的回忆恢复到了1892年的春天。在下一幅从遗忘的迷雾中浮现出来的画面中，我看到了自己居住在巴黎的和平旅馆。当我的大脑正在经受痛苦折磨的时候，我收到了一封急件，我的妈妈生命垂危。我一刻都没有耽搁，日夜兼程返回家乡，几个星期之后，她去世了。值得注意的是，这段时期之后，我完全沉浸在自己的研究主题之中，我能回忆起最微小的细节和最无关紧要的观察，甚至还能背诵一些文本和复杂的数学公式。

我的信念是：一切皆有补偿，只要付出就有回报，真正的回报与付出的劳动和牺牲成正比例，因此我对自己所有的发明都充满信心。在我看来，放大发射机对于未来的几代人来说是最为重要和最有价值的。关于这一预测,并不是基于它所必然带来的商业和工业革命的考虑,而且也是因为它会给人类带来诸多成就。它的成就不仅仅体现在应用价值,而且也体现在能够推动文明的进步,前者与后者相比,显得微不足道。我们面临的问题不仅仅是丰富的物质存在就能够解决的。相反,这方面的进展充满了危险,如同生来就极为贫穷痛苦一样严重。如果我们释放出原子能量,或者发现了其他更为廉价、更加不受限制的能量,在任何时间、任何地点、任何程度而言,这都不是祝福,而是将给人类带来灾难,导致纠纷和无政府状态,最终导致仇恨现政权力量的出现。最大的好处来自趋于统一与和谐的技术进步,而我的无线发射机正是如此。它的意义在于,人类的声音和肖像将被复制到任何地方;工厂的动力可能来自千里之外的瀑布驱动的能量;空中的机器将围绕地球无休止地运行;太阳能得以控制,可以用来创造湖泊与河流,于是沙漠得以被改造成肥沃的土壤。由此带来的电报、电话和类似的使用将自动切除静态和其他形式的干扰,这些干扰是目前无线电应用面临的主要障碍。

  这是一个急需讨论的话题,几句话是说不清楚的。在过去的10年里面,一些人傲慢地宣称,他们已经成功地克服了这些障碍。在他们公布出自己的成果之后,我仔细地检查了他们的设计，并对其中的大多数进行了实际检验，但结果都是负面的。最近来自美国海军部的官方声明，可能会给那些轻易上当受骗的新闻编辑上一堂课，教会他们如何辨别这些声明的真伪。基本的情况是，这些发现都建立在非常荒唐的理论基础之上，所以每当它们呈现在我的面前时，我只能一笑而过。最近，又有人宣布出现了一个新发现，宣传声势非常浩大，但是结果可想而知，又是虎头蛇尾，夸大其词。

这让我想起了几年前发生的一件激动人心的事情，当时我正在进行高频电流的实验。史蒂夫·布罗迪刚从布鲁克林的大桥上跳下来，许多人都在模仿这一壮举，跳桥已经成为一种庸俗的行为，但是其第一份报道确实轰动了整个纽约市。我对此印象深刻，经常和人谈论这位勇敢的印刷商人。在一个非常炎热的下午，我感到自己需要呼吸新鲜空气，于是来到了一个酒吧，当时该城市类似的酒吧大约有3万个，我点了一份美味饮料，其酒精含量大约为20%，这种饮料现在几乎没有了，只有到欧洲贫穷落后的国家才可以找到。当时，该场所人数众多，我并不引人注目，人们在讨论问题的时候，我无意中说出了一句话，却引起了在场人士的极度震惊，我说的是："这就是我跳桥的时候所说的话。"我刚说完这些话，就感觉自己像德国诗人席勒诗歌中所提到的提摩太一样，马上拥有了众多的追随者。刹那间，人群一片混乱，10几个声音同时喊道："看，他是布罗迪！"我把25美分的硬币扔在柜台上，迅速跑向门口，但是人们都跟着我，喊道："拦住史蒂夫！"很多人因此产生了误会，试图抓住我，我疯狂地寻找避难所。幸运的是，我疯狂地逃过了拐角，通过一个消防通道，回到了实验室，我迅速脱掉外套，把自己伪装成一个正在工作的铁匠，开始干起活来。事实证明，这种伪装是不必要的，我已经躲避开了那些人。很多年之后，在晚上难以入睡的时候，我时常回想起那天的麻烦，如果那些人抓住我，并且发现我不是史蒂夫·布罗迪，那么结果会怎么样呢？

现在，有一位工程师在某个技术机构中做了一场演讲，宣称基于"迄今为止未知的自然法则"，找到了一个新奇的方案，能够处理静电学的问题。他争辩说静电的扰动是向上和向下传播的，同时发射器产生的电流会沿着地球表面传播。这种观点非常荒唐，就如同我的那次经历一样。他的声明意味着被大气层包裹的地球就像是一个冷凝器，能够充电，也能够放电，其方式与每一本物理学教科书中的基本原理都是相矛盾的。即使在富兰克林时代，这种假设也极为荒谬，众所周知的事实是，大气的电流和机器电流是相同的。显然，自然和人工扰动以完全相同的方式在地面和空气中传播，同时在水平和垂直方向上都设置了电动势，任何类似工程师提出的方法都不可能克服干扰。事实是这样的：在空气中，潜在的上升速度是每上升50英尺，增加50伏左右，天线的上下端之间存在2万到4万伏特的压差。带电的大气团一直在运动，把电能断断续续地传输给导体，于是在敏感的电话接收器那里产生了摩擦噪声。终端越高，导线所包含的空间越大，噪声就越大，但它必须纯粹是局部的现象，与真正的麻烦无关。

1900年，我开始对自己的无线系统进行完善。它安有4个天线，它们被仔细地校准到相同的频率，并与众多的物体相连接，以方便从任何方向接收的信号都能产生放大作用。当我想确定传输的脉冲的来源时，每个对角位置的传输脉冲都是串联在一个初级线圈上的，用能量检测线路。在前一种情况下，电话里的声音很大；在后一种情况里面，正如所预料的那样，是没有声音的。两个天线彼此综合，但是真正的静力学在两种情况下都会发挥作用，在这两种情况下，我必须设计出体现不同原理的特别预防方法。

就像我很久以前所建议的那样，使用连接到地面上两点的接收器，由带电的空气引起的麻烦将得到解决，这一问题在现在建造的结构中非常严重。此外，由于回路的不同特性，各种干扰的强度也会减少到一半左右。这是完全不言自明的，但是对于一些思维比较简单的无线电用户来说，仍然具有一定的启示作用，他们的经验仅仅局限于设备的形式，认为这是用斧子就可以加以改进的，这就等于还没有把熊杀死，就要除去熊皮。如果情况的确如此，无线干扰确实非常混乱，那么就可以使用无天线接收的方式解决这些问题。然而，事实是，要符合这样的条件，埋在地下的电线必须是绝缘的，它比在空中垂直放置更容易受到外来脉冲的影响。公平地说，确实已经取得了一丁点儿的进展，但并非特定方法或者装置的改善。它仅仅是通过放弃巨大的结构而实现的，该结构在传输上效果极为糟糕，整体不适合于接收，也不适用于找到更为精准的接收位置。正如我在之前的一篇文章中所指出的那样，要处理掉这一困难，使其变好，必须在系统中做出彻底的改变，而且变化越早，效果越好。

事实上，如果在这一切还处于起步阶段的时候，即包括专家在内的绝大多数人对于最终的可能性完全没有概念的时候，就匆忙地通过立法结构使其形成政府垄断，结果将是灾难性的。这是几个星期前由丹尼尔斯部长提出的。毫无疑问，这位杰出的官员以真诚的信念向参议院和众议院提出了他的呼吁。但普遍的证据清楚地表明，最好的结果总是在健康的商业竞争之中得到。

然而，无线网络应该得到充分的发展自由，还存在特殊的原因。首先，在人类历史上，它为人类生活的改善提供了比其他任何发明或发现更大、更重要的前景。随后，我们还必须明白，这种奇妙的艺术完全是在美国本土进化的，可以被称为"美国人的创造"，它比电话、白炽灯或飞机更应该拥有专利。有胆识的新闻机构和股票批发商在传播错误信息方面如此成功，以至于即使是如此优秀的期刊，也像《科学美国人》（Scientific American）一样把主要功劳归功于某个外国。当然，德国人给了我们赫兹波，俄国、英国、法国和意大利的专家很快就用它们来做信号控制。这是对于新介质的明显运用，而且使用的是旧的、古典的和没有改进的感应线圈，不是新型的反光通信法。传播的半径是非常有限的，结果几乎没有什么价值，而赫兹振荡作为一种传递信息的手段，可以被我在1891年所提倡的声波所取代。所有这些尝试都是在无线系统原理基本完成后的三年内完成的，今天被普遍使用，在美国，它的强大工具性能已经被清楚地描述和发展。这些赫兹的电器和方法至今没有留下痕迹。我们正朝着相反的方向前进，我们所取得的成就应该归功于这个国家人民的智慧和努力。基本专利已经过期，机会对所有人开放。这位部长的主要观点是基于干扰理论的。根据7月29日《纽约先驱报》上对于部长声明的报道,一个强大的发电站发出的信号可以在世界上每个村庄被拦截。鉴于这一事实,在美国实行限制是没有什么用处的,我在1900年的实验中已经证明了这一点,

关于这一点,我想说的是,最近,一个长相古怪的绅士拜访了我,希望说服我在遥远的地方建立世界发射机。"我们没有钱,"他说道,"但是我们可以给你大量的黄金,数量你可以自己选择。"我告诉他,我想首先看看我的发明在美国能做些什么,就这样结束了会见。但是,我很满意一些黑暗力量在起作用,随着时间的推移,持续的通信将变得更加困难。唯一的补救办法就是不受干扰的系统。它已经被完善,所要做的只是要把它投入使用。

可怕的暴力冲突仍然是人们最为关注的问题,也许最重要的是放大发射机可能作为攻击和防御的机器,特别是它将与遥控力学结合在一起。这项发明是我少年时代就开始的观察的逻辑结果,并一直延续在我的生活之中。当第一个结果发表时,《电气评论》的评论是,它将成为"人类进步和推动文明最有力的因素之一"。这一预言的实现,时间不会太过遥远。在1898年和1900年,它被提供给政府并且可能被采纳。如果他们想要亚历山大的恩惠时,那么我就将要去寻找亚历山大的牧羊人。那时,我真的

以为它会消灭战争，因为它具有无限的破坏性，能够排除战斗的人为因素。尽管目前我对它的潜力没有失去信心，但我的观点已经发生了改变。

除非引发战争的物质因素被完全根除，否则战争是不可避免的，而这是我们星球冲突的主要原因。只有各方面的分歧都被消除，情报的传送、旅客的运输、能源的供应和传输，才将在未来的某一天得以实现，从而确保友好关系的永久性。我们现在最希望的是地球上的个人和社区之间更紧密的联系，彼此更好地理解，消除对民族利己主义和傲慢的崇高理想的狂热崇拜，这总是倾向于将世界带入原始的野蛮和冲突中。任何联盟或议会的行动都不会阻止这样的灾难。这些只是让弱者受制于强者的新手段。

我在14年前就已经在这方面做了介绍，当时一些主要的政府组成了神圣的联盟——是由已故的安德鲁·卡内基倡导的，他可能被认为是这个想法之父，给了它更多的宣传和动力。在总统的努力之前，还有其他人也在宣传这一思想。虽然不能否认这样一项协定可能对一些不幸的人有物质上的好处，但它不能达到所要求的主要目标。和平只能是普遍的启蒙和融合的自然结果。在种族上，我们离幸福的实现还很遥远。

今日的世界，仍然存在巨大的冲突，我坚信，如果美国坚持自己的传统，不卷入"纠缠不清的联盟"，人类的利益将得到最大的满足。这个国家地理位置优越，远离即将到来的冲突的战场，没有任何领土扩张的动力，拥有取之不竭的资源和充足的人口，充满了自由和权利的精神，处于一种独特的优势地位。因此，它能够独立地发挥其巨大的物质实力和道德力量，使其比作为一个联盟的成员能够更有效地发挥作用。

在《电气实验》杂志上发表的一篇小传里，我回忆了自己早期生活的环境，与此相伴的是一种令我不断进行想象和自我反省的痛苦。这种精神活动，起初是在疾病和痛苦的压力下不由自主地进行的，逐渐变成了第二天性，最终使我认识到，我是一个没有自由意志的自动机，在思想和行动上，仅仅是对环境的力量做出反应。我们的身体结构如此复杂，我们的动作方式如此之多，外部印象对我们感觉器官的刺激如此微妙和难以捉摸，以至于普通人很难理解这一事实。然而，对于训练有素的研究者来说，没有什么比300年前笛卡尔所理解和提出的机械论更有说服力。但在他的时代，我们的机体的许多重要功能都是未知的，特别是在光线的性质、眼睛的构造和运作方面，哲学家们都处于黑暗之中，我对此一无所知。

近年来，科学研究在这些领域取得了长足的进步。关于这一观点，许多作品已经出版，也没有什么值得怀疑的了。最能干、最有说服力的倡导者之一，也许是曾经担任巴斯德的助理的菲利克斯·勒·丹特克（Felix Le Dantec）。他做了一系列著名的关于向日性的实验，非常清晰地确立了低端生物体之中光线控制的模式，他最近的著作《被迫的运动》给人以很多启示。科学界的人接受了这个理论，就像其他任何被认可的理论一样。但是对于我来说，这是一个真理，我每时每刻都在用我的行为和思想来证明它。外在印象激发了我的身体和思维的活动，并且一直停留在我的脑海之中。只有在非常罕见的情况下，当我处于异常专注的状态时，我才发现很难找到最初的冲动。

大部分人都没有意识到外部世界和自身所产生的联系，数百万未成年人因此患病而过早离去。最常见的日常事件似乎神秘而又令人费解。一个人可能会突然感到一阵悲伤，并在他的大脑中寻找一个解释，他可能已经注意到它是由一朵云遮住了太阳的光线造成的。当某人在街上遇见某个朋友或在某个地方看到朋友照片的时候，他会觉得很奇怪。当他失去一个领扣时，会对自己的动作进行一小时的梳理和咒骂，因为他无法想象自己之前的动作，也无法直接定位纽扣究竟掉在了哪里。缺乏观察仅仅是无知的一种形式，并且是盛行的许多病态的观念和愚蠢的想法的根源。每十个人中就有一个不相信心灵感应和其他灵能表现、唯心主义和能够与死者交流，他们拒绝倾听有心或者无意的欺骗。

为了说明这种趋势在美国头脑清醒的人群中根深蒂固，我可能会提到一个滑稽的事件。战争爆发前不久，我的涡轮机展览在这座城市引起了广泛的评论，它们发表在技术杂志上，我预料制造商们会展开对这项发明的争夺，我期盼来自底特律的那个人为此进行专门的设计，他拥有积累百万财富的不可思议的能力。

印有特斯拉头像的纸币

我自信地认为他总有一天会出现，我把这事告诉了我的秘书和助手。果然，在一个晴朗的早晨，福特汽车公司的一群工程师向我提出了一项重要的计划。"我没告诉你吗？"我得意地对我的员工说，"你真了不起，特斯拉先生；一切都如你所料。" 这些人一坐下来，我当然立即开始称赞这美妙的东西，一位发言人打断我说："我们都知道这一切，但我们正在做一件特别的事情。我们已经建立了一个研究心理现象的心理学会，我们希望你加入我们的行列。"我猜想那些工程师可能永远都不知道，他们差点儿被我赶出办公室。

从那时起，一些那个时代最伟大的人物，包括科学界的领军人物，他们曾经创造了不朽的成就，他们称赞我拥有一种不寻常的思想，于是我把自己所有的思考能力都集中在解决重大问题上，完全不考虑付出的问题。多年来，我一直在努力解开死亡之谜，热切地注视着各种精神灵异的现象。但在我生存的过程中，只有一次，我有过让自己觉得超自然的经历，那发生在我母亲去世的时候。

当时，我因为疼痛和长时间的失眠而精疲力竭，一天晚上，我被带到离我们家大约两个街区的地方。我躺在那里，感觉迷茫而绝望，我想如果我的母亲在我离开的时候去世，她必然会给我发出一个信号。两三个月前，我和我已故的朋友威廉·克劳克斯爵士在伦敦讨论唯灵论的时候，我受到了这些思想的影响。我可能很少受到他人的影响，但对他的观点却深信不疑，因为他曾经在辐射问题上进行了划时代的工作，我在学生时代读过他的著作，这让我开始从事电气职业。我想，我的母亲是一个天才的女人，在直觉的力量上尤其出色。整个夜晚，我大脑中的每根纤维都处于高度紧张的状态，但是什么都没有发生。直到第二天凌晨，我可能睡着了，也可能是昏昏欲睡的状态，突然间，我看到云彩带着不可思议的一群美丽的天使飘浮而来，其中一位天使深情地看着我，然后逐渐呈现出我母亲的特征。慢慢地，她飘过房间，我被一种难以形容的甜美歌声唤醒。在那一瞬间，我发现我的母亲刚刚去世了。事实的确如此。我无法理解我预先收到的痛苦感知的意义，于是在身体健康状况不佳的情况下给威廉·克劳克斯爵士写了一封信。

当我恢复的时候，我花费了很长一段时间寻找这一奇怪的表现的外在原因，令我感到欣慰的是，在经过了几个月的努力之后，我终于成功了。我曾看过一幅著名艺术家的画，画的是在某个季节里面，一群天使飘浮在空中，这震撼了我。这就是我梦中出现的景象，只是没有和我妈妈一样的天使而已。当时，还有音乐来自附近教堂的合唱团，那正是复活节的早晨，所有这一切看似巧合，却又符合科学的事实。

这都是很久以前的事情了，此后我再也没有改变自己对心理学和灵异论的看法，虽然它没有任何的基础。对于这一切的信仰是智力自然发展的结果。宗教教条不再局限于正统的意义，但每一个个体都信奉某种至高无上的力量。我们都必须有一个理想来管理我们的行为和确保内心的满足。无论它是一种信仰、艺术、科学或其他任何东西，只要它履行了一种非物化力的功能，形式就不那么重要了。作为一个整体，某个共同的观念应该被普遍接受，这对人类和平的存在是至关重要的。

虽然我没有得到任何证据来支持心理学家和唯灵论者的论点。但我已经证明了生命具有自动的特征，这不只是通过对个人行为的连续观察，更确切地说，是来自总结概括。我认为这是人类社会最伟大的时刻，我将对此进行短暂简要的介绍。当我很年轻的时候，就对这个惊人的事实有了初步了解，但多年以来，我把我所注意到的仅仅看作是巧合。换句话说，无论何时，或者是我自己，或者是我所依附的某个人，或者是我全心奉献的事业，被他人以一种特殊的方式伤害，人们普遍会认为这非常不公平，是无法想象的事情，我会经历一种奇特的、无法定义的痛苦。但是，我很快找到了一个更恰当的词汇——"宇宙"，不久之后，那些伤害我的人也会遇到痛苦。在许多这样的案例之后，我向一些朋友倾诉了这个问题，这提供了一个机会，他们得以了解理论的真相，可以表述成如下的文字：

我们的身体构造相似，受到同样的外部影响。这导致相同的反应，总体活动的协调一致，于是我们的社会规则和法律才得以确立起来。我们全受控于媒介的力量，就像在水面上的瓶塞一样，易于把来自外部环境的影响看作自己的自由意志。我们所做的运动都是生命的防腐剂，是为了维持生命的运转，人们看起来彼此独立，但是被无形的联系连接起来。只要生物体处于完美的状态，它就能准确地对外部刺激做出回应，但在任何个体中，都存在一些紊乱的时刻，导致他的自我保护能力受损。

当然，每个人都明白，如果一个人变聋了，他的视力变弱了，或者他的四肢受伤了，那么他继续生存的机会就减少了。还有一个事实，也许更确切地说，大脑中的某些缺陷，使自动反应或多或少地丧失了这种重要的品质，并导致其迅速走向毁灭。一个非常敏感和善于观察的人，他高度发达的机制都完好无损，能够精确地依据环境变化采取行动，于是他就能够超越纯粹的机械，使他能够逃避太微妙而未能被察觉的危险。当他与控制器官完全错误的人接触时，这种感觉开始发挥作用，他就会感受到"宇宙"带给他的痛苦。该真相已经被数百次证明，我正在邀请其他学习自然学科的学生把注意力集中在这个问题上，相信通过综合和系统的努力，将会给世界带来不可估量的价值。

为了验证我的理论，我很早就产生了建造自动机的想法，但是直到在1893年开始无线电研究的时候，才开始付诸实践。在接下来的两三年里面，我发明了远距离控制的自动装置，在我的实验室里面展出。1896年，我设计了一台能够进行多种操作的完整机器，但是直到1897年才彻底改制完毕。关于这台机器，我在1900年6月的《世纪》杂志上发表的文章以及当时的其他期刊上都有插图和描述，1898年初的时候，它创造了一种我的发明从来没有过的轰动效应。1898年11月，我得到了一项关于新技术的基本专利，但只有在主考官来到纽约并对机器进行了展示之后，我的申请才得以通过，因为他们以前认为这是不可思议的。我记得，后来我拜访了华盛顿的一位官员，准备把这项发明提供给政府，当我告诉他我所取得的成就时，他突然大笑起来。那时没有人相信这种装置会如此完善。不幸的是，在申请这个专利的时候，依据我私人律师的建议，我指出控制是通过一个单一电路的媒介和一个众所周知的探测器得以进行的，所以我没有保护我的方法和设备的个性化。事实上，我的船是通过几个电路的联合作用控制的，各种干扰都被排除在外。更为普遍的意义在于，我使用循环的方式接收电路，包括冷凝器，因为我的高压发射机电离了大厅里的空气，所以即使是很小的天线也能从周围的空气中吸收几个小时的电。

举个例子，我发现了一个灯泡，直径为12英寸，它已经被过度使用了，其中一个单独的终端连接上了一个很短的电线，它会连续不断地闪烁1 000次，才能将实验室中空气里面的电量彻底耗尽。接收器的环路形式对这样的干扰不敏感，很奇怪的是，它在最近的时候变得流行起来。事实上，它所收集的能量要比天线或一根长接地的电线要少得多，但它确实会消除现有无线设备固有的一些缺陷。我在观众面前展示发明的时候，要求参观者能够提出一些问题，对于涉及的问题，这个自动装置就会发出信号进行回答。当时的人们认为这是一件神奇的事情，其实原理非常简单，是我本人在利用这个装置回答问题。

与此同时，我打造了另一艘比较大型的遥控船只，它的照片被刊登在《电气实验》的杂志上。船只是由线圈控制的，电线在船体上围绕了几圈，它是完全不透水的，所以可以放置到水中。该仪器与第一个装置非常相似，除了一些个别的特性之外，例如，我引进了白炽灯，这样人们就能够看到机器的运转状态。

这些机器在操纵者的视野范围之内进行控制，它们是我设想的遥控力学的第一步，也是极为粗糙的步骤。下一个符合逻辑的改进目标就是，把它应用于超越视线范围之外的自动机制，并与控制中心有很大的距离。我一直提倡把它们应用为战争的武器，能够取代枪支。现在看来，无论如何，这个问题的重要性似乎得到了承认，这一点从媒体的随意报道中可以看出来，它们声称该发明很特别，但是没有任何创新。虽然媒体对此并不乐观，但是能够引起关注已经足矣。它虽然并不完美，但仍然具有可行性，现有的无线电站，能够控制飞机，使它遵循一定的大致路线展开运动，能够执行几百英里以外的操

特斯拉

作。这种机器也可以用几种方式进行机械控制，我对此毫不怀疑。它可能在战争中有一些用处。但是，据我所知，目前还没有哪一种工具能够以精确的方式完成这种操作。我花了数年的时间研究这个问题，并且已经发明出一些方法，应该能够创造出更大的奇迹。

如前所述，当我还在大学就读的时候，我设计了一种和现在的飞机不一样的飞行器。其基本原理是正确的，但却不能付诸实践，主要是因为缺乏足够大的原动力进行驱动。近年来，我已经成功地克服了这一障碍，我正在规划的飞行器，没有机翼、副翼、螺旋桨和其他外部附件，它将具有极快的速度，极有可能在不久的将来为和平提供有力的支撑。这种飞机，完全由反应驱动，我曾经讲述过，它是由机械或无线能量进行控制的。通过安装适当的装置，将导弹通过空中投放到指定的地点（可能在数千英里之外）是切实可行的。但我们不会就此止步，远程自动机最终将被生产出来，它将拥有自己的智能，它们的到来将会带来一场革命。早在1898年，我就向一个大型制造企业的代表提出了一个问题，即进行自动运载装置的展览，它将执行一系列类似于判断的操作。但当时我的建议被认为是空想，没有任何结果。

目前，很多聪明能干的人正在设计应急的手段，试图防止可怕冲突的重演,这场冲突只是在理论上结束了,我在1914年12月20日的《太阳报》上发表的一篇文章已经正确地预言了冲突的持续时间和主要问题。建立国际联盟的提议并不是一个补救方法,相反,在一些有远见的人士看来,这可能会带来事与愿违的后果。令人感到遗憾的是,在为了维持和平所设计的框架之内,却采取了惩罚性的政策,几年之后,国家之间的战争可能没有军队,不需要军舰和枪炮,而是采用更为可怕、更具有杀伤力的武器,其作战范围也可能完全没有限制。一座城市,无论距离敌人多么遥远,都可以被敌人摧毁,而且地球上的任何力量都无法阻止他这样做。如果我们想要避免一场即将到来的灾难和一种可能把这个地球变成地狱的状态,就应该推动飞行机器的发展和无线能量的传输,不能有丝毫的拖延,并且需要动员国家所有的力量和资源。

附录 尼古拉·特斯拉年谱

1856年7月10日，尼古拉·特斯拉出生在克罗地亚斯米湾村一个塞族家庭，父母都是塞尔维亚人，他是五个孩子中的老四。

1875年，在奥地利的格拉茨科技大学修读电机工程。

1880年，毕业于布拉格大学。

1882年，他继爱迪生发明直流电（DC）后不久，即发明了交流电（AC），并制造出世界上第一台交流电发电机，并始创多相传电技术。

1884年，移民美国成为美国公民，并获取耶鲁大学及哥伦比亚大学名誉博士学位。

1887年，创建了自己的公司——特斯拉电灯与电气制造公司。

1888年，发展了特斯拉线圈的原理。

1891年，证实了无限能量传输。

1893—1895年，研究高频交流电，制造了第一台无线电发射机。

1895年，替美国尼加拉瓜发电站制造发电机组，致使该发电站至今仍是世界著名水电站之一。

1897年，使马可尼的无线电通信理论成为现实。

1898年，发明无线电遥控技术并取得专利（美国专利号码#613.809）。

1899年，发现了X光（X-Ray）摄影技术。

1906年，在他的50岁生日之际，特斯拉示范了他的200匹马力（约150千瓦），每分钟一千五百转的无叶片涡轮。

1908年6月30日，通古斯大爆炸。

1912年，拒绝和爱迪生共享诺贝尔物理学奖。

1943年1月7日，尼古拉·特斯拉与世长辞，享年87岁，终生未娶。

My Inventions:
Nikola Tesla's Autobiography

At the age of 63 Tesla tells the story of his creative life. First published in 1919 in the Electrical Experimenter magazine.

I.
My Early Life

The progressive development of man is vitally dependent on invention. It is the most important product of his creative brain. Its ultimate purpose is the complete mastery of mind over the material world, the harnessing of the forces of nature to human needs. This is the difficult task of the inventor who is often misunderstood and unrewarded. But he finds ample compensation in the pleasing exercises of his powers and in the knowledge of being one of that exceptionally privileged class without whom the race would have long ago perished in the bitter struggle against pitiless elements.

Speaking for myself, I have already had more than my full measure of this exquisite enjoyment, so much that for many years my life was little short of continuous rapture. I am credited with being one of the hardest workers and perhaps I am, if thought is the equivalent of labor, for I have devoted to it almost all of my waking hours. But if work is interpreted to be a definite performance in a specified time according to a rigid rule, then I may be the worst of idlers. Every effort under compulsion demands a sacrifice of life-energy. I never paid such a price. On the contrary, I have thrived on my thoughts.

In attempting to give a connected and faithful account of my activities in this series of articles, I must dwell, however reluctantly, on the impressions of my youth and the circumstances and events which have been instrumental in determining my career.

Our first endeavors are purely instinctive, promptings of an imagination vivid and undisciplined. As we grow older reason asserts itself and we become more and more systematic and designing. But those early impulses, thó not immediately productive, are of the greatest moment and may shape our very destinies. Indeed, I feel now that had I understood and cultivated instead of suppressing them, I would have added substantial value to my bequest to the world. But not until I had attained manhood did I realize that I was an inventor.

This was due to a number of causes. In the first place I had a brother who was gifted to an extraordinary degree—one of those rare phenomena of mentality which biological investigation has failed to explain. His premature death left my parents disconsolate.

We owned a horse which had been presented to us by a dear friend. It was a magnificent animal of Arabian breed, possessed of almost human intelligence, and was cared for and petted by the whole family, having on one occasion saved my father's life under remarkable circumstances. My father had been called one winter night to perform an urgent duty and while crossing the mountains, infested by wolves, the horse became frightened and ran away, throwing him violently to the ground. It arrived home bleeding and exhausted, but after the alarm was sounded immediately dashed off again, returning to the spot, and before the searching party were far on the way they were met by my father, who had recovered consciousness and remounted, not realizing that he had been lying in the snow for several hours. This horse was responsible for my brother's injuries from which he died. I witnessed the tragic scene and altho fifty-six years have elapsed since, my visual impression of it has lost none of its force. The recollection of his attainments made every effort of mine seem dull in comparison.

Anything I did that was creditable merely caused my parents to feel their loss more keenly. So I grew up with little confidence in myself. But I was far from being considered a stupid boy, if I am to judge from an incident of which I have still a strong remembrance. One day the Aldermen were passing thru a street where I was at play with other boys. The oldest of these venerable gentlemen—a wealthy citizen—paused to give a silver piece to each of us. Coming to me he suddenly stopt and commanded, "Look in my eyes." I met his gaze, my hand outstretched to receive the much valued coin, when, to my dismay, he said, "No, not much, you can get nothing from me, you are too smart."

They used to tell a funny story about me. I had two old aunts with wrinkled faces, one of them having two teeth protruding like the tusks of an elephant which she buried in my cheek every time she kissed me. Nothing would scare me more than the prospect of being hugged by these as affectionate as unattractive relatives. It happened that while being carried in my mother's arms they asked me who was the prettier of the two. After examining their faces intently, I answered thoughtfully, pointing to one of them, "This here is not as ugly as the other."

Then again, I was intended from my very birth for the clerical profession and this thought constantly oppressed me. I longed to be an engineer but my father was inflexible. He was the son of an officer who served in the army of the Great Napoleon and, in common with his brother, professor of mathematics in a prominent institution, had received a military education but, singularly enough, later embraced the clergy in which vocation he achieved eminence. He was a very erudite man, a veritable natural philosopher, poet and writer and his sermons were said to be as eloquent as those of Abraham a Sancta-Clara. He had a prodigious memory and frequently recited at length from works in several languages. He often remarked playfully that if some of the classics were lost he could restore them. His style of writing was much admired. He penned sentences short and terse and was full of wit and satire. The humorous remarks he made were always peculiar and characteristic. Just to illustrate, I may mention one or two instances.

Among the help there was a cross-eyed man called Mane,

employed to do work around the farm. He was chopping wood one day. As he swung the axe my father, who stood nearby and felt very uncomfortable, cautioned him, "For God's sake, Mane, do not strike at what you are looking but at what you intend to hit."

On another occasion he was taking out for a drive a friend who carelessly permitted his costly fur coat to rub on the carriage wheel. My father reminded him of it saying, "Pull in your coat, you are ruining my tire."

He had the odd habit of talking to himself and would often carry on an animated conversation and indulge in heated argument, changing the tone of his voice. A casual listener might have sworn that several people were in the room.

Altho I must trace to my mother's influence whatever inventiveness I possess, the training he gave me must have been helpful. It comprised all sorts of exercises—as, guessing one another's thoughts, discovering the defects of some form or expression, repeating long sentences or performing mental calculations. These daily lessons were intended to strengthen memory and reason and especially to develop the critical sense, and were undoubtedly very beneficial.

My mother descended from one of the oldest families in the country and a line of inventors. Both her father and grandfather originated numerous implements for household, agricultural and other uses. She was a truly great woman, of rare skill, courage and fortitude, who had braved the storms of life and past thru many a trying experience. When she was sixteen a virulent pestilence swept the country. Her father was called away to administer the last sacraments to the dying and during his absence she went alone to the assistance of a neighboring family who were stricken by the dread disease. All of the members, five in number, succumbed in rapid succession. She bathed, clothed and laid out the bodies, decorating them with flowers according to the custom of the country and when her father returned he found everything ready for a Christian burial.

My mother was an inventor of the first order and would, I believe, have achieved great things had she not been so remote from modern life and its multifold opportunities. She invented and constructed all kinds of tools and devices and wove the finest designs from thread which was spun by her. She even planted the seeds, raised the plants and separated the fibers herself. She worked indefatigably, from break of day till late at night, and most of the wearing apparel and furnishings of the home was the product of her hands. When she was past sixty, her fingers were still nimble enough to tie three knots in an eyelash.

There was another and still more important reason for my late awakening. In my boyhood I suffered from a peculiar affliction due to the appearance of images, often accompanied by strong flashes of light, which marred the sight of real objects and interfered with my thought and action. They were pictures of things and scenes which I had really seen, never of those I imagined. When a word was spoken to me the image of the object it designated would present itself vividly to my vision and sometimes I was quite unable to distinguish whether what I saw was tangible or not. This caused me great discomfort and anxiety. None of the students of psychology or physiology whom I have consulted could ever explain satisfactorily these phenomena. They seem to have been unique altho I was probably predisposed as I know that my brother experienced a similar trouble. The theory I have formulated is that the images were the result of a reflex action from the brain on the retina under great excitation. They certainly were not hallucinations such as are produced in diseased and anguished minds, for in other respects I was normal and composed. To give an idea of my distress, suppose that I had witnessed a funeral or some such nerve-racking spectacle. Then, inevitably, in the stillness of night, a vivid picture of the scene would thrust itself before my eyes and persist despite all my efforts to banish it. Sometimes it would even remain fixt in space tho I pushed my hand thru it. If my explanation is correct, it should be able to project on a screen the image of any object one conceives and make it visible. Such an advance would revolutionize all human relations. I am convinced that this wonder can and will be accomplished in time to come; I may add that I have devoted much thought to the solution of the problem.

To free myself of these tormenting appearances, I tried to concentrate my mind on something else I had seen, and in this way I would of ten obtain temporary relief; but in order to get it I had to conjure continuously new images. It was not long before I found that I had exhausted all of those at my command; my "reel" had run out, as it were, because I had seen little of the world—only objects in my home and the immediate surroundings. As I performed these mental operations for the second or third time, in order to chase the appearances from my vision, the remedy gradually lost all its force. Then I instinctively commenced to make excursions beyond the limits of the small world of which I had knowledge, and I saw new scenes. These were at first very blurred and indistinct, and would flit away when I tried to concentrate my attention upon them, but by and by I succeeded in fixing them; they gained in strength and distinctness and finally assumed the concreteness of real things. I soon discovered that my best comfort was attained if I simply went on in my vision farther and farther, getting new impressions all the time, and so I began to travel—of course, in my mind. Every night (and sometimes during the day), when alone, I would start on my journeys—see new places, cities and countries—live there, meet people and make friendships and acquaintances and, however unbelievable, it is a fact that they were just as dear to me as those in actual life and not a bit less intense in their manifestations.

This I did constantly until I was about seventeen when my thoughts turned seriously to invention. Then I observed to my delight that I could visualize with the greatest facility. I needed no models, drawings or experiments. I could picture them all as real in my mind. Thus I have been led unconsciously to evolve what I consider a new method of materializing inventive concepts and ideas, which is radically opposite to the purely experimental and is in my opinion ever so much more expeditious and efficient.

The moment one constructs a device to carry into practise a crude idea he finds himself unavoidably engrossed with the details and defects of the apparatus. As he goes on improving and reconstructing, his force of concentration diminishes and he loses sight of the great underlying principle. Results may be obtained but always at the sacrifice of quality. My method is different. I do not rush into actual work. When I get an idea I start at once building it up in my imagination. I change the construction, make improvements and operate the device in my mind. It is absolutely immaterial to me whether I run my turbine in thought or test it in my shop. I even note if it is out of balance. There is no difference whatever, the results are the same. In this way I am able to rapidly develop and perfect a conception without touching anything. When I have gone so far as to embody in the invention every possible improvement I can think of and see no fault anywhere, I put into concrete form this final product of my brain. Invariably my device works as I conceived that it should, and the experiment comes out exactly as I planned it. In twenty years there has not been a single exception. Why should it be otherwise? Engineering, electrical and mechanical, is positive in results. There is scarcely a subject that cannot be mathematically treated and the effects calculated or the results determined beforehand from the available theoretical and practical data. The carrying out into practise of a crude idea as is being generally done is, I hold, nothing but a waste of energy, money and time.

My early affliction had, however, another compensation. The incessant mental exertion developed my powers of observation and enabled me to discover a truth of great importance. I had noted that the appearance of images was always preceded by actual vision of scenes under peculiar and generally very exceptional conditions and I was impelled on each occasion to locate the original impulse. After a while this effort grew to be almost automatic and I gained great facility in connecting cause and effect. Soon I became aware, to my surprise, that every thought I conceived was suggested by an external impression.Not only this but all my actions were prompted in a similar way. In the course of time it became perfectly evident to me that I was merely an automaton endowed with power of movement, responding to the stimuli of the sense organs and thinking and acting accordingly.The practical result of this was the art of telautomatics which has been so far carried out only in an imperfect manner. Its latent possibilities will, however, be eventually shown. I have been since years planning self-controlled automata and believe that mechanisms can be produced which will act as if possessed of reason, to a limited degree, and will create a revolution in many commercial and industrial departments.

I was about twelve years old when I first succeeded in banishing an image from my vision by wilful effort, but I never had any control over the flashes of light to which I have referred. They were, perhaps, my strangest experience and inexplicable. They usually occurred when I found myself in a dangerous or distressing situation, or when I was greatly exhilarated.In some instances I have seen all the air around me filled with tongues of living flame. Their intensity, instead of diminishing, increased with time and seemingly attained a maximum when I was about twenty-five years old.

While in Paris, in 1883, a prominent French manufacturer sent me an invitation to a shooting expedition which I accepted. I had been long confined to the factory and the fresh air had a wonderfully invigorating effect on me. On my return to the city that night I felt a positive sensation that my brain had caught fire. I saw a light as tho a small sun was located in it and I past the whole night applying cold compressions to my tortured head. Finally the flashes diminished in frequency and force but it took more than three weeks before they wholly subsided. When a second invitation was extended to me my answer was an emphatic NO!

These luminous phenomena still manifest themselves from time to time, as when a new idea opening up possibilities strikes me, but they are no longer exciting, being of relatively small intensity. When I close my eyes I invariably observe first, a background of very dark and uniform blue, not unlike the sky on a clear but starless night. In a few seconds this field becomes animated with innumerable scintillating flakes of green, arranged in several layers and advancing towards me. Then there appears, to the right, a beautiful pattern of two systems of parallel and closely spaced lines, at right angles to one another, in all sorts of colors with yellow–green and gold predominating. Immediately thereafter the lines grow brighter and the whole is thickly sprinkled with dots of twinkling light. This picture moves slowly across the field of vision and in about ten seconds vanishes to the left, leaving behind a ground of rather unpleasant and inert grey which quickly gives way to a billowy sea of clouds, seemingly trying to mould themselves in living shapes. It is curious that I cannot project a form into this grey until the second phase is reached. Every time, before falling asleep, images of persons or objects flit before my view. When I see them I know that I am about to lose consciousness. If they are absent and refuse to come, it means a sleepless night.

To what an extent imagination played a part in my early life I may illustrate by another odd experience. Like most children I was fond of jumping and developed an intense desire to support myself in the air. Occasionally a strong wind richly charged with oxygen blew from the mountains rendering my body as light as cork and then

I would leap and float in space for a long time. It was a delightful sensation and my disappointment was keen when later I undeceived myself.

During that period I contracted many strange likes, dislikes and habits, some of which I can trace to external impressions while others are unaccountable. I had a violent aversion against the earrings of women but other ornaments, as bracelets, pleased me more or less according to design. The sight of a pearl would almost give me a fit but I was fascinated with the glitter of crystals or objects with sharp edges and plane surfaces. I would not touch the hair of other people except, perhaps, at the point of a revolver. I would get a fever by looking at a peach and if a piece of camphor was anywhere in the house ,it caused me the keenest discomfort. Even now I am not insensible to some of these upsetting impulses. When I drop little squares of paper in a dish filled with liquid, I always sense a peculiar and awful taste in my mouth. I counted the steps in my walks and calculated the cubical contents of soup plates, coffee cups and pieces of food— otherwise my meal was unenjoyable. All repeated acts or operations I performed had to be divisible by three and if I mist I felt impelled to do it all over again, even if it took hours.

Up to the age of eight years, my character was weak and vacillating. I had neither courage or strength to form a firm resolve. My feelings came in waves and surges and vibrated unceasingly between extremes. My wishes were of consuming force and like the heads of the hydra, they multiplied. I was oppressed by thoughts of pain in life and death and religious fear. I was swayed by superstitious belief and lived in constant dread of the spirit of evil, of ghosts and ogres and other unholy monsters of the dark. Then, all at once, there came a tremendous change which altered the course of my whole existence.

Of all things I liked books the best. My father had a large library and whenever I could manage I tried to satisfy my passion for reading. He did not permit it and would fly into a rage when he caught me in the act. He hid the candles when he found that I was reading in secret. He did not want me to spoil my eyes. But I obtained tallow, made the wicking and cast the sticks into tin forms, and every night I would bush the keyhole and the cracks and read, often till dawn, when all others slept and my mother started on her arduous daily task.

On one occasion I came across a novel entitled "Abafi" (*the Son of Aba*), a Serbian translation of a well known Hungarian writer, Josika. This work somehow awakened my dormant powers of will and I began to practise self-control. At first my resolutions faded like snow in April, but in a little while I conquered my weakness and felt a pleasure I never knew before—that of doing as I willed.

In the course of time this vigorous mental exercise became second nature. At the outset my wishes had to be subdued but gradually desire and will grew to be identical.After years of such discipline I gained so complete a mastery over myself that I toyed with passions which have meant destruction to some of the strongest men. At a certain age I contracted a mania for gambling which greatly worried my parents. To sit down to a game of cards was for me the quintessence of pleasure. My father led an exemplary life and could not excuse the senseless waste of time and money in which I indulged. I had a strong resolve but my philosophy was bad. I would say to him, "I can stop whenever I please but is it worth while to give up that which I would purchase with the joys of Paradise?" On frequent occasions he gave vent to his anger and contempt but my mother was different. She understood the character of men and knew that one's salvation could only be brought about thru his own efforts. One afternoon, I remember, when I had lost all my money and was craving for a game, she came to me with a roll of bills and said, "Go and enjoy yourself. The sooner you lose all we possess the better it will be. I know that you will get over it." She was right. I conquered my passion then and there and only regretted that it had not been a hundred times as strong. I not only vanquished but tore it from my heart so as not to leave even a trace of desire. Ever since that time I have been as indifferent to any form of gambling as to picking teeth.

During another period I smoked excessively, threatening to ruin my health. Then my will asserted itself and I not only stopt but destroyed all inclination. Long ago I suffered from heart trouble until I discovered that it was due to the innocent cup of coffee I consumed every morning. I discontinued at once, tho I confess it was not an easy task.In this way I checked and bridled other habits and passions and have not only preserved my life but derived an immense amount of satisfaction from what most men would consider privation and sacrifice.

After finishing the studies at the Polytechnic Institute and University I had a complete nervous breakdown and while the malady lasted I observed many phenomena strange and unbelievable.

II.
My First Efforts At Invention

I shall dwell briefly on these extraordinary experiences, on account of their possible interest to students of psychology and physiology and also because this period of agony was of the greatest consequence on my mental development and subsequent labors. But it is indispensable to first relate the circumstances and conditions which preceded them and in which might be found their partial explanation.

From childhood I was compelled to concentrate attention upon myself. This caused me much suffering but, to my present view, it was a blessing in disguise for it has taught me to appreciate the inestimable value of introspection in the preservation of life, as well as a means of achievement. The pressure of occupation and the incessant stream of impressions pouring into our consciousness thru all the gateways of knowledge make modern existence hazardous in many ways. Most persons are so absorbed in the contemplation of the outside world that they are wholly oblivious to what is passing on within themselves. The premature death of millions is primarily traceable to this cause. Even among those who exercise care it is a common mistake to avoid imaginary, and ignore the real dangers. And what is true of an individual also applies, more or less, to a people as a whole.

Witness, in illustration, the prohibition movement. A drastic, if not unconstitutional, measure is now being put thru in this country to prevent the consumption of alcohol and yet it is a positive fact that coffee, tea, tobacco, chewing gum and other stimulants, which are freely indulged in even at the tender age, are vastly more injurious to the national body, judging from the number of those who succumb. So, for instance, during my student years I gathered from the published necrologues in Vienna, the home of coffee drinkers, that deaths from heart trouble sometimes reached sixty-seven percent of the total. Similar observations might probably be made in cities where the consumption of tea is excessive. These delicious beverages superexcite and gradually exhaust the fine fibers of the brain. They also interfere seriously with arterial circulation and should be enjoyed all the more sparingly as their deleterious effects are slow and imperceptible. Tobacco, on the other hand, is conducive to easy and pleasant thinking and detracts from the intensity and concentration necessary to all original and vigorous effort of the intellect. Chewing gum is helpful for a short while but soon drains the glandular system and inflicts irreparable damage, not to speak of the revulsion it creates. Alcohol in small quantities is an excellent tonic, but is toxic in its action when absorbed in larger amounts, quite immaterial as to whether it is taken in as whiskey or produced in the stomach from sugar. But it should not be overlooked that all these are great eliminators assisting Nature, as they do, in upholding her stern but just law of the survival of the fittest. Eager reformers should also be mindful of the eternal perversity of mankind which makes the indifferent "laissez–faire" by far preferable to enforced restraint.

The truth about this is that we need stimulants to do our best work under present living conditions, and that we must exercise moderation and control our appetites and inclinations in every direction. That is what I have been doing for many years, in this way maintaining myself young in body and mind.

Abstinence was not always to my liking but I find ample reward in the agreeable experiences I am now making. Just in the hope of converting some to my precepts and convictions I will recall one or two.

A short time ago I was returning to my hotel. It was a bitter cold night, the ground slippery, and no taxi to be had. Half a block behind me followed another man, evidently as anxious as myself to get under cover. Suddenly my legs went up in the air. In the same instant there was a flash in my brain, the nerves responded, the muscles contracted, I swung thru 180 degrees and landed on my hands. I resumed my walk as tho nothing had happened when the stranger caught up with me.

"How old are you?" he asked, surveying me critically.

"Oh, about fifty-nine," I replied. "What of it?"

"Well," said he, "I have seen a cat do this but never a man."

About a month since I wanted to order new eyeglasses and went to an oculist who put me thru the usual tests. He looked at me incredulously as I read off with ease the smallest print at considerable distance. But when I told him that I was past sixty he gasped in astonishment.

Friends of mine often remark that my suits fit me like gloves but they do not know that all my clothing is made to measurements which were taken nearly 35 years ago and never changed. During this same period my weight has not varied one pound. In this connection I may tell a funny story.

One evening, in the winter of 1885, Mr. Edison, Edward H. Johnson, the President of the Edison Illuminating Company, Mr. Batchellor, Manager of the works, and myself entered a little place opposite 65 Fifth Avenue where the offices of the company were located. Someone suggested guessing weights and I was induced to step on a scale. Edison felt me all over and said: "Tesla weighs 152 lbs. to an ounce," and he guest it exactly. Stript I weighed 142 lbs. and that is still my weight. I whispered to Mr. Johnson: "How is it possible that Edison could guess my weight so closely?"

"Well," he said, lowering his voice. "I will tell you, confidentially, but you must not say anything. He was employed for a long time in a Chicago slaughter–house where he weighed thousands of hogs every day! That's why."

My friend, the Hon. Chauncey M. Depew, tells of an Englishman on whom he sprung one of his original anecdotes and who listened with a puzzled expression but a year later laughed out loud. I will frankly confess it took me longer than that to appreciate Johnson's joke.

Now, my well being is simply the result of a careful and measured mode of living and perhaps the most astonishing thing is that three times in my youth I was rendered by illness a hopeless physical wreck and given up by physicians. More than this, thru ignorance and lightheartedness, I got into all sorts of difficulties, dangers and scrapes from which I extricated myself as by enchantment. I was almost drowned a dozen times; was nearly boiled alive and just mist being cremated. I was entombed, lost and frozen. I had hair-breadth escapes from mad dogs, hogs, and other wild animals. I past thru dreadful diseases and met with all kinds of odd mishaps and that I am hale and hearty today seems like a miracle. But as I recall these incidents to my mind I feel convinced that my preservation was not altogether accidental.

An inventor's endeavor is essentially lifesaving. Whether he harnesses forces, improves devices, or provides new comforts and conveniences, he is adding to the safety of our existence. He is also better qualified than the average individual to protect himself in peril, for he is observant and resourceful. If I had no other evidence that I was, in a measure, possessed of such qualities I would find it in these personal experiences. The reader will be able to judge for himself if I mention one or two instances.

On one occasion, when about 14 years old, I wanted to scare some friends who were bathing with me. My plan was to dive under a long floating structure and slip out quietly at the other end. Swimming and diving came to me as naturally as to a duck and I was confident that I could perform the feat. Accordingly I plunged into the water and, when out of view, turned around and proceeded rapidly towards the opposite side. Thinking that I was safely beyond the structure, I rose to the surface but to my dismay struck a beam. Of course, I quickly dived and forged ahead with rapid strokes until my breath was beginning to give out. Rising for the second time, my head came again in contact with a beam.Now I was becoming desperate.

However, summoning all my energy, I made a third frantic attempt but the result was the same. The torture of suppress breathing was getting unendurable, my brain was reeling and I felt myself sinking. At that moment, when my situation seemed absolutely hopeless, I experienced one of those flashes of light and the structure above me appeared before my vision. I either discerned or guest that there was a little space between the surface of the water and the boards resting on the beams and, with consciousness nearly gone, I floated up, prest my mouth close to the planks and managed to inhale a little air, unfortunately mingled with a spray of water which nearly choked me. Several times I repeated this procedure as in a dream until my heart, which was racing at a terrible rate, quieted down and I gained composure. After that I made a number of unsuccessful dives, having completely lost the sense of direction, but finally succeeded in getting out of the trap when my friends had already given me up and were fishing for my body.

That bathing season was spoiled for me thru recklessness but I soon forgot the lesson and only two years later I fell into a worse predicament. There was a large flour mill with a dam across the river near the city where I was studying at that time. As a rule the height of the water was only two or three inches above the dam and to swim out to it was a sport not very dangerous in which I often indulged. One day I went alone to the river to enjoy myself as usual. When I was a short distance from the masonry, however, I was horrified to observe that the water had risen and was carrying me along swiftly. I tried to get away but it was too late. Luckily, tho, I saved myself from being swept over by taking hold of the wall with both hands. The pressure against my chest was great and I was barely able to keep my head above the surface. Not a soul was in sight and my voice was lost in the roar of the fall. Slowly and gradually I became exhausted and unable to withstand the strain longer. Just as I was about to let go, to be dashed against the rocks below, I saw in a flash of light a familiar diagram illustrating the hydraulic principle that the pressure of a fluid in motion is proportionate to the area exposed, and automatically I turned on my left side.As if by magic the pressure was reduced and I found it comparatively easy in that position to resist the force of the stream. But the danger still confronted me. I knew that sooner or later I would be carried down, as it was not possible for any help to reach me in time, even if I attracted attention. I am ambidextrous now but then I was lefthanded and had comparatively little strength in my right arm. For this reason I did not dare to turn on the other side to rest and nothing remained but to slowly push my body along the dam. I had to get away from the mill towards which my face was turned as the current there was much swifter and deeper. It was a long and painful ordeal and I came near to failing at its very end for I was confronted with a depression in the masonry. I managed to get over with the last ounce of my force and fell in a swoon when I reached the bank, where I was found. I had torn virtually all the skin from my left side and it took several weeks before the fever subsided and I was well. These are only two of many instances but they may be sufficient to show that had it not been for the inventor's instinct I would not have lived to tell this tale.

Interested people have often asked me how and when I began to invent. This I can only answer from my present recollection in the light of which the first attempt I recall was rather ambitious for it involved the invention of an apparatus and a method. In the former I was anticipated but the latter was original. It happened in this way.

One of my playmates had come into the possession of a hook and fishing-tackle which created quite an excitement in the village, and the next morning all started out to catch frogs. I was left alone and deserted owing to a quarrel with this boy. I had never seen a real hook and pictured it as something wonderful, endowed with peculiar qualities, and was despairing not to be one of the party. Urged by necessity, I somehow got hold of a piece of soft iron wire, hammered the end to a sharp point between two stones, bent it into shape, and fastened it to a strong string. I then cut a rod, gathered some bait, and went down to the brook where there were frogs in abundance. But I could not catch any and was almost discouraged when it occurred to me to dangle the empty hook in front of a frog sitting on a stump. At first he collapsed but by and by his eyes bulged out and became bloodshot, he swelled to twice his normal size and made a vicious snap at the hook.

Immediately I pulled him up. I tried the same thing again and again and the method proved infallible. When my comrades, who in spite of their fine outfit had caught nothing, came to me they were green with envy. For a long time I kept my secret and enjoyed the monopoly but finally yielded to the spirit of Christmas. Every boy could then do the same and the following summer brought disaster to the frogs.

In my next attempt I seem to have acted under the first instinctive impulse which later dominated me—to harness the energies of nature to the service of man. I did this thru the medium of May-bugs – or June-bugs as they are called in America—which were a veritable pest in that country and sometimes broke the branches of trees by the sheer weight of their bodies. The bushes were black with them. I would attach as many as four of them to a crosspiece, ratably arranged on a thin spindle, and transmit the motion of the same to a large disc and so derive considerable "power". These creatures were remarkably efficient, for once they were started they had no sense to stop and continued whirling for hours and hours and the hotter it was the harder they worked. All went well until a strange boy came to the place. He was the son of a retired officer in the Austrian Army. That urchin ate May-bugs alive and enjoyed them as tho they were the finest blue-point oysters. That disgusting sight terminated my endeavors in this promising field and I have never since been able to touch a May-bug or any other insect for that matter.

After that, I believe, I undertook to take apart and assemble the clocks of my grandfather. In the former operation I was always successful but often failed in the latter. So it came that he brought my work to a sudden halt in a manner not too delicate and it took thirty years before I tackled another clockwork again.

Shortly there after I went into the manufacture of a kind of pop-gun which comprised a hollow tube, a piston, and two plugs of hemp. When firing the gun, the piston was prest against the stomach and the tube was pushed back quickly with both hands. The air between the plugs was compressed and raised to high temperature and one of them was expelled with a loud report. The art consisted in selecting a tube of the proper taper from the hollow stalks. I did very well with that gun but my activities interfered with the window panes in our house and met with painful discouragement.

If I remember rightly, I then took to carving swords from pieces of furniture which I could conveniently obtain. At that time I was under the sway of the Serbian national poetry and full of admiration for the feats of the heroes. I used to spend hours in mowing down my enemies in the form of corn–stalks which ruined the crops and netted me several spankings from my mother. Moreover these were not of the formal kind but the genuine article.

I had all this and more behind me before I was six years old and had past thru one year of elementary school in the village of Smiljan where I was born. At this juncture we moved to the little city of Gospic nearby. This change of residence was like a calamity to me. It almost broke my heart to part from our pigeons, chickens and sheep, and our magnificent flock of geese which used to rise to the clouds in the morning and return from the feeding grounds at sundown in battle formation, so perfect that it would have put a squadron of the best aviators of the present day to shame. In our new house I was but a prisoner, watching the strange people I saw thru the window blinds. My bashfulness was such that I would rather have faced a roaring lion than one of the city dudes who strolled about. But my hardest trial came on Sunday when I had to dress up and attend the service. There I meet with an accident, the mere thought of which made my blood curdle like sour milk for years afterwards. It was my second adventure in a church. Not long before I was entombed for a night in an old chapel on an inaccessible mountain which was visited only once a year. It was an awful experience, but this one was worse.

There was a wealthy lady in town, a good but pompous woman, who used to come to the church gorgeously painted up and attired with an enormous train and attendants. One Sunday I had just finished ringing the bell in the belfry and rushed downstairs when this grand dame was sweeping out and I jumped on her train. It tore off with a ripping noise which sounded like a salvo of musketry fired by raw recruits. My father was livid with rage. He gave me a gentle slap on the cheek, the only corporal punishment he ever administered to me but I almost feel it now. The embarrassment and confusion that followed are indescribable. I was practically ostracised until something else happened which redeemed me in the estimation of the community.

An enterprising young merchant had organized a fire department. A new fire engine was purchased, uniforms provided and the men drilled for service and parade. The engine was, in reality, a pump to be worked by sixteen men and was beautifully painted red and black. One afternoon the official trial was prepared for and the machine was transported to the river. The entire population turned out to witness the great spectacle. When all the speeches and ceremonies were concluded, the command was given to pump, but not a drop of water came from the nozzle. The professors and experts tried in vain to locate the trouble. The fizzle was complete when I arrived at the scene. My knowledge of the mechanism was nil and I knew next to nothing of air pressure, but instinctively I felt for the suction hose in the water and found that it had collapsed. When I waded in the river and opened it up the water rushed forth and not a few Sunday clothes were spoiled. Archimedes running naked thru the streets of Syracuse and shouting Eureka at the top of his voice did not make a greater impression than myself. I was carried on the shoulders and was the hero of the day.

Upon settling in the city I began a four-years' course in the so-called Normal School preparatory to my studies at the College or Real Gymnasium. During this period my boyish efforts and exploits, as well as troubles, continued. Among other things I attained the unique distinction of champion crow catcher in the country. My method of procedure was extremely simple. I would go in the forest, hide in the bushes, and imitate the call of the bird. Usually I would get several answers and in a short while a crow would flutter down into the shrubbery near me. After that all I needed to do was to throw a piece of cardboard to distract its attention, jump up and grab it before it could extricate itself from the undergrowth. In this way I would capture as many as I desired. But on one occasion something occurred which made me respect them. I had caught a fine pair of birds and was returning home with a friend. When we left the forest, thousands of crows had gathered making a frightful racket. In a few minutes they rose in pursuit and soon enveloped us. The fun lasted until all of a sudden I received a blow on the back of my head which knocked me down. Then they attacked me viciously. I was compelled to release the two birds and was glad to join my friend who had taken refuge in a cave.

In the schoolroom there were a few mechanical models which interested me and turned my attention to water turbines. I constructed many of these and found great pleasure in operating them. How extraordinary was my life an incident may illustrate. My uncle had no use for this kind of pastime and more than once rebuked me. I was fascinated by a description of Niagara Falls I had perused, and pictured in my imagination a big wheel run by the Falls. I told my uncle that I would go to America and carry out this scheme. Thirty years later I saw my ideas carried out at Niagara and marveled at the unfathomable mystery of the mind.

I made all kinds of other contrivances and contraptions but among these the arbalists I produced were the best. My arrows, when shot, disappeared from sight and at close range traversed a plank of pine one inch thick. Thru the continuous tightening of the bows I developed skin on my stomach very much like that of a crocodile and I am often wondering whether it is due to this exercise that I am able even now to digest cobble–stones!

Nor can I pass in silence my performances with the sling which would have enabled me to give a stunning exhibit at the Hippodrome. And now I will tell of one of my feats with this antique implement of war which will strain to the utmost the credulity of the reader. I was practicing while walking with my uncle along the river. The sun was setting, the trout were playful and from time to time one would shoot up into the air, its glistening body sharply defined against a projecting rock beyond. Of course any boy might have hit a fish under these propitious conditions but I undertook a much more difficult task and I foretold to my uncle, to the minutest detail, what I intended doing. I was to hurl a stone to meet the fish, press its body against the rock, and cut it in two. It was no sooner said than done. My uncle looked at me almost scared out of his wits and exclaimed "Vade retro Satanas!" and it was a few days before he spoke to me again. Other records, how ever great, will be eclipsed but I feel that I could peacefully rest on my laurels for a thousand years.

III.
My Later Endeavors:
The Discovery of the Rotating Magnetic Field

At the age of ten I entered the Real Gymnasium which was a new and fairly well equipt institution. In the department of physics were various models of classical scientific apparatus, electrical and mechanical. The demonstrations and experiments performed from time to time by the instructors fascinated me and were undoubtedly a powerful incentive to invention. I was also passionately fond of mathematical studies and often won the professor's praise for rapid calculation. This was due to my acquired facility of visualizing the figures and performing the operations, not in the usual intuitive manner, but as in actual life. Up to a certain degree of complexity it was absolutely the same to me whether I wrote the symbols on the board or conjured them before my mental vision. But freehand drawing, to which many hours of the course were devoted, was an annoyance I could not endure. This was rather remarkable as most of the members of the family excelled in it. Perhaps my aversion was simply due to the predilection I found in undisturbed thought. Had it not been for a few exceptionally stupid boys, who could not do anything at all, my record would have been the worst. It was a serious handicap as under the then existing educational regime, drawing being obligatory, this deficiency threatened to spoil my whole career and my father had considerable trouble in railroading me from one class to another.

In the second year at that institution I became obsessed with the idea of producing continuous motion thru steady air pressure. The pump incident, of which I have told, had set afire my youthful imagination and imprest me with the boundless abilities of a vacuum. I grew frantic in my desire to harness this inexhaustible energy but for a long time I was groping in the dark. Finally, however, my endeavors crystallized in an invention which was to enable me to achieve what no other mortal ever attempted.

Imagine a cylinder freely rotatable on two bearings and partly surrounded by a rectangular trough which fits it perfectly. The open side of the trough is closed by a partition so that the cylindrical segment within the enclosure divides the latter into two compartments entirely separated from each other by air-tight sliding joints. One of these compartments being sealed and once for all exhausted, the other remaining open, a perpetual rotation of the cylinder would result, at least, I thought so. A wooden model was constructed and fitted with infinite care and when I applied the pump on one side and actually observed that there was a tendency to turning, I was delirious with joy.

Mechanical flight was the one thing I wanted to accomplish altho still under the discouraging recollection of a bad fall I sustained by jumping with an umbrella from the top of a building. Every day I used to transport myself thru the air to distant regions but could not understand just how I managed to do it. Now I had something concrete—a flying machine with nothing more than a rotating shaft, flapping wings, and—a vacuum of unlimited power! From that time on I made my daily aerial excursions in a vehicle of comfort and luxury as might have befitted King Solomon. It took years before I understood that the atmospheric pressure acted at right angles to the surface of the cylinder and that the slight rotary effort I observed was due to a leak. Tho this knowledge came gradually it gave me a painful shock.

I had hardly completed my course at the Real Gymnasium when I was prostrated with a dangerous illness or rather, a score of them, and my condition became so desperate that I was given up by physicians. During this period I was permitted to read constantly, obtaining books from the Public Library which had been neglected and entrusted to me for classification of the works and preparation of the catalogues. One day I was handed a few volumes of new literature unlike anything I had ever read before and so captivating as to make me utterly forget my hopeless state. They were the earlier works of Mark Twain and to them might have been due the miraculous recovery which followed. Twenty-five years later, when I met Mr. Clemens and we formed a friendship between us, I told him of the experience and was amazed to see that great man of laughter burst into tears.

My studies were continued at the higher Real Gymnasium in Carlstadt, Croatia, where one of my aunts resided. She was a distinguished lady, the wife of a Colonel who was an old war-horse having participated in many battles. I never can forget the three years I past at their home. No fortress in time of war was under a more rigid discipline. I was fed like a canary bird. All the meals were of the highest quality and deliciously prepared but short in quantity by a thousand percent. The slices of ham cut by my aunt were like tissue paper. When the Colonel would put something substantial on my plate she would snatch it away and say excitedly to him: "Be careful, Niko is very delicate." I had a voracious appetite and suffered like Tantalus.

But I lived in an atmosphere of refinement and artistic taste quite unusual for those times and conditions. The land was low and marshy and malaria fever never left me while there despite of the enormous amounts of quinin I consumed. Occasionally the river would rise and drive an army of rats into the buildings, devouring everything even to the bundles of the fierce paprika. These pests were to me a welcome diversion.I thinned their ranks by all sorts of means, which won me the unenviable distinction of rat-catcher in the community. At last, however, my course was completed, the misery ended, and I obtained the certificate of maturity which brought me to the cross-roads.

During all those years my parents never wavered in their resolve to make me embrace the clergy, the mere thought of which filled me with dread. I had become intensely interested in electricity under the stimulating influence of my Professor of Physics, who was an ingenious man and often demonstrated the principles by apparatus of his own invention. Among these I recall a device in the shape of a freely rotatable bulb, with tinfoil coatings, which was made to spin rapidly when connected to a static machine. It is impossible for me to convey an adequate idea of the intensity of feeling I experienced in witnessing his exhibitions of these mysterious phenomena. Every impression produced a thousand echoes in my mind. I wanted to know more of this wonderful force; I longed for experiment and investigation and resigned myself to the inevitable with aching heart.

Just as I was making ready for the long journey home I received word that my father wished me to go on a shooting expedition. It was a strange request as he had been always strenuously opposed to this kind of sport. But a few days later I learned that the cholera was raging in that district and, taking advantage of an opportunity, I returned to Gospic in disregard of my parents' wishes. It is incredible how absolutely ignorant people were as to the causes of this scourge which visited the country in intervals of from fifteen to twenty years. They thought that the deadly agents were transmitted thru the air and filled it with pungent odors and smoke. In the meantime they drank the infected water and died in heaps. I contracted the awful disease on the very day of my arrival and altho surviving the crisis, I was confined to bed for nine months with scarcely any ability to move. My energy was completely exhausted and for the second time I found myself at death's door.

In one of the sinking spells which was thought to be the last, my father rushed into the room. I still see his pallid face as he tried to cheer me in tones belying his assurance. "Perhaps," I said, "I may get well if you will let me study engineering." "You will go to the best technical institution in the world," he solemnly replied, and I knew that he meant it. A heavy weight was lifted from my mind but the relief would have come too late had it not been for a marvelous cure brought about thru a bitter decoction of a peculiar bean. I came to life like another Lazarus to the utter amazement of everybody.

My father insisted that I spend a year in healthful physical outdoor exercises to which I reluctantly consented. For most of this term I roamed in the mountains, loaded with a hunter's outfit and a bundle of books, and this contact with nature made me stronger in body as well as in mind. I thought and planned, and conceived many ideas almost as a rule delusive. The vision was clear enough but the knowledge of principles was very limited. In one of my inventions I proposed to convey letters and packages across the seas, thru a submarine tube, in spherical containers of sufficient strength to resist the hydraulic pressure. The pumping plant, intended to force the water thru the tube, was accurately figured and designed and all other particulars carefully worked out. Only one trifling detail, of no consequence, was lightly dismist. I assumed an arbitrary velocity of the water and, what is more, took pleasure in making it high, thus arriving at a stupendous performance supported by faultless calculations. Subsequent reflections, however, on the resistance of pipes to fluid flow determined me to make this invention public property.

Another one of my projects was to construct a ring around the equator which would, of course, float freely and could be arrested in its spinning motion by reactionary forces, thus enabling travel at a rate of about one thousand miles an hour, impracticable by rail. The reader will smile. The plan was difficult of execution, I will admit, but not nearly so bad as that of a well-known New York professor, who wanted to pump the air from the torrid to the temperate zones, entirely forgetful of the fact that the Lord had provided a gigantic machine for this very purpose.

Still another scheme, far more important and attractive, was to derive power from the rotational energy of terrestrial bodies. I had discovered that objects on the earth's surface, owing to the diurnal rotation of the globe, are carried by the same alternately in and against the direction of translatory movement. From this results a great change in momentum which could be utilized in the simplest imaginable manner to furnish motive effort in any habitable region of the world. I cannot find words to describe my disappointment when later I realized that I was in the predicament of Archimedes, who vainly sought for a fixt point in the universe.

At the termination of my vacation I was sent to the Polytechnic School in Gratz, Styria, which my father had chosen as one of the oldest and best reputed institutions. That was the moment I had eagerly awaited and I began my studies under good auspices and firmly resolved to succeed. My previous training was above the average, due to my father's teaching and opportunities afforded. I had acquired the knowledge of a number of languages and waded thru the books of several libraries, picking up information more or less useful. Then again, for the first time, I could choose my subjects as I liked, and free-hand drawing was to bother me no more.

I had made up my mind to give my parents a surprise, and during the whole first year I regularly started my work at three o'clock in the morning and continued until eleven at night, no Sundays or holidays excepted. As most of my fellow-students took thinks easily, naturally enough I eclipsed all records. In the course of that year I past thru nine exams and the professors thought I deserved more than the highest qualifications. Armed with their flattering certificates, I went home for a short rest, expecting a triumph, and was mortified when my father made light of these hard won honors. That almost killed my ambition; but later, after he had died, I was pained to find a package of letters which the professors had written him to the effect that unless he took me away from the Institution I would be killed thru overwork.

Thereafter I devoted myself chiefly to physics, mechanics and mathematical studies, spending the hours of leisure in the libraries. I had a veritable mania for finishing whatever I began, which often got me into difficulties. On one occasion I started to read the works of Voltaire when I learned, to my dismay, that there were close on one hundred large volumes in small print which that monster had written while drinking seventy-two cups of black coffee per diem. It had to be done, but when I laid aside the last book I was very glad, and said, "Never more!"

My first year's showing had won me the appreciation and friendship of several professors. Among these were Prof. Rogner, who was teaching arithmetical subjects and geometry; Prof. Poeschl, who held the chair of theoretical and experimental physics, and Dr. Alle, who taught integral calculus and specialized in differential equations. This scientist was the most brilliant lecturer to whom I ever listened. He took a special interest in my progress and would frequently remain for an hour or two in the lecture room, giving me problems to solve, in which I delighted. To him I explained a flying machine I had conceived, not an illusionary invention, but one based on sound, scientific principles, which has become realizable thru my turbine and will soon be given to the world. Both Professors Rogner and Poeschl were curious men. The former had peculiar ways of expressing himself and whenever he did so there was a riot, followed by a long and embarrassing pause. Prof. Poeschl was a methodical and thoroly grounded German. He had enormous feet and hands like the paws of a bear, but all of his experiments were skillfully performed with lock-like precision and without a miss.

It was in the second year of my studies that we received a Gramme dynamo from Paris, having the horseshoe form of a laminated field magnet, and a wire-wound armature with a commutator. It was connected up and various effects of the currents were shown. While Prof. Poeschl was making demonstrations, running the machine as a motor, the brushes gave trouble, sparking badly, and I observed that it might be possible to operate a motor without these appliances. But he declared that it could not be done and did me the honor of delivering a lecture on the subject, at the conclusion of which he remarked: "Mr. Tesla may accomplish great things, but he certainly never will do this. It would be equivalent to converting a steadily pulling force, like that of gravity, into a rotary effort. It is a perpetual motion scheme, an impossible idea." But instinct is something which transcends knowledge. We have, undoubtedly, certain finer fibers that enable us to perceive truths when logical deduction, or any other willful effort of the brain, is futile.For a time I wavered, imprest by the professor's authority, but soon became convinced I was right and undertook the task with all the fire and boundless confidence of youth.

I started by first picturing in my mind a direct-current machine, running it and following the changing flow of the currents in the armature. Then I would imagine an alternator and investigate the processes taking place in a similar manner. Next I would visualize systems comprising motors and generators and operate them in various ways.The images I saw were to me perfectly real and tangible. All my remaining term in Gratz was passed in intense but fruitless efforts of this kind, and I almost came to the conclusion that the problem was insolvable.

In 1880 I went to Prague, Bohemia, carrying out my father's wish to complete my education at the University there. It was in that city that I made a decided advance, which consisted in detaching the commutator from the machine and studying the phenomena in this new aspect, but still without result. In the year following there was a sudden change in my views of life. I realized that my parents had been making too great sacrifices on my account and resolved to relieve them of the burden. The wave of the American telephone had just reached the European continent and the system was to be installed in Budapest, Hungary. It appeared an ideal opportunity, all the more as a friend of our family was at the head of the enterprise. It was here that I suffered the complete breakdown of the nerves to which I have referred.

What I experienced during the period of that illness surpasses all belief. My sight and hearing were always extraordinary. I could clearly discern objects in the distance when others saw no trace of them. Several times in my boyhood I saved the houses of our neighbors from fire by hearing the faint crackling sounds which did not disturb their sleep, and calling for help. In 1899, when I was past forty and carrying on my experiments in Colorado, I could hear very distinctly thunderclaps at a distance of 550 miles. The limit of audition for my young assistants was scarcely more than 150 miles. My ear was thus over thirteen times more sensitive. Yet at that time I was, so to speak, stone deaf in comparison with the acuteness of my hearing while under the nervous strain. In Budapest I could hear the ticking of a watch with three rooms between me and the time-piece. A fly alighting on a table in the room would cause a dull thud in my ear. A carriage passing at a distance of a few miles fairly shook my whole body. The whistle of a locomotive twenty or thirty miles away made the bench or chair on which I sat vibrate so strongly that the pain was unbearable. The ground under my feet trembled continuously. I had to support my bed on rubber cushions to get any rest at all. The roaring noises from near and far often produced the effect of spoken words which would have frightened me had I not been able to resolve them into their accidental components. The sun's rays, when periodically intercepted, would cause blows of such force on my brain that they would stun me. I had to summon all my will power to pass under a bridge or other structure as I experienced a crushing pressure on the skull. In the dark I had the sense of a bat and could detect the presence of an object at a distance of twelve feet by a peculiar creepy sensation on the forehead. My pulse varied from a few to two hundred and sixty beats and all the tissues of the body quivered with twitchings and tremors which was perhaps the hardest to bear. A renowned physician who gave me daily large doses of Bromide of Potassium pronounced my malady unique and incurable.

It is my eternal regret that I was not under the observation of experts in physiology and psychology at that time.I clung desperately to life, but never expected to recover. Can anyone believe that so hopeless a physical wreck could ever be transformed into a man of astonishing strength and tenacity, able to work thirty–eight years almost without a day's interruption, and find himself still strong and fresh in body and mind? Such is my case. A powerful desire to live and to continue the work, and the assistance of a devoted friend and athlete accomplished the wonder. My health returned and with it the vigor of mind. In attacking the problem again I almost regretted that the struggle was soon to end. I had so much energy to spare. When I undertook the task it was not with a resolve such as men often make. With me it was a sacred vow, a question of life and death. I knew that

I would perish if I failed. Now I felt that the battle was won. Back in the deep recesses of the brain was the solution, but I could not yet give it outward expression.

One afternoon, which is ever present in my recollection, I was enjoying a walk with my friend in the City Park and reciting poetry. At that age I knew entire books by heart, word for word. One of these was Goethe's Faust. The sun was just setting and reminded me of the glorious passage:

"Sie ruckt und weicht, der Tag ist uberlebt,

Dort eilt sie hin und fordert neues Leben.

Oh, dass kein Flugel mich vom Boden hebt

Ihr nach und immer nach zu streben!

Ein schoner Traum indessen sie entweicht,

Ach, zu des Geistes Flugeln wird so leicht

Kein korperlicher Flugel sich gesellen!"

[The glow retreats, done is the day of toil;

It yonder hastes, new fields of life exploring;

Ah, that no wing can lift me from the soil

Upon its track to follow, follow soaring!

A glorious dream! though now the glories fade.

Alas! the wings that lift the mind no aid

Of wings to lift the body can bequeath me.]

As I uttered these inspiring words the idea came like a flash of lightning and in an instant the truth was revealed. I drew with a stick on the sand the diagrams shown six years later in my address before the American Institute of Electrical Engineers, and my companion understood them perfectly. The images I saw were wonderfully sharp and clear and had the solidity of metal and stone, so much so that I told him: "See my motor here; watch me reverse it." I cannot begin to describe my emotions. Pygmalion seeing his statue come to life could not have been more deeply moved. A thousand secrets of nature which I might have stumbled upon accidentally I would have given for that one which I had wrested from her against all odds and at the peril of my existence.

IV.
The Discovery of the Tesla Coil and Transformer

For a while I gave myself up entirely to the intense enjoyment of picturing machines and devising new forms. It was a mental state of happiness about as complete as I have ever known in life. Ideas came in an uninterrupted stream and the only difficulty I had was to hold them fast. The pieces of apparatus I conceived were to me absolutely real and tangible in every detail, even to the minute marks and signs of wear. I delighted in imagining the motors constantly running, for in this way they presented to mind's eye a more fascinating sight. When natural inclination develops into a passionate desire, one advances towards his goal in seven–league boots. In less than two months I evolved virtually all the types of motors and modifications of the system which are now identified with my name. It was, perhaps, providential that the necessities of existence commanded a temporary halt to this consuming activity of the mind.

I came to Budapest prompted by a premature report concerning the telephone enterprise and, as irony of fate willed it, I had to accept a position as draftsman in the Central Telegraph Office of the Hungarian Government at a salary which I deem it my privilege not to disclose! Fortunately, I soon won the interest of the Inspector-in-Chief and was thereafter employed on calculations, designs and estimates in connection with new installations, until the Telephone Exchange was started, when I took charge of the same. The knowledge and practical experience I gained in the course of this work was most valuable and the employment gave me ample opportunities for the exercise of my inventive faculties. I made several improvements in the Central Station apparatus and perfected a telephone repeater or amplifier which was never patented or publicly described but would be creditable to me even today. In recognition of my efficient assistance the organizer of the undertaking, Mr. Puskas, upon disposing of his business in Budapest, offered me a position in Paris which I gladly accepted.

I never can forget the deep impression that magic city produced on my mind. For several days after my arrival I roamed thru the streets in utter bewilderment of the new spectacle. The attractions were many and irresistible, but, alas, the income was spent as soon as received. When Mr. Puskas asked me how I was getting along in the new sphere, I described the situation accurately in the statement that "the last twenty-nine days of the month are the toughest!" I led a rather strenuous life in what would now be termed "Rooseveltian fashion." Every morning, regardless of weather, I would go from the Boulevard St. Marcel, where I resided, to a bathing house on the Seine, plunge into the water, loop the circuit twenty-seven times and then walk an hour to reach Ivry, where the Company's factory was located. There I would have a woodchopper's breakfast at half-past seven o'clock and then eagerly await the lunch hour, in the meanwhile cracking hard nuts for the Manager of the Works, Mr. Charles Batchellor, who was an intimate friend and assistant of Edison. Here I was thrown in contact with a few Americans who fairly fell in love with me because of my proficiency in billiards. To these men I explained my invention and one of them, Mr. D. Cunningham, Foreman of the Mechanical Department, offered to form a stock company. The proposal seemed to me comical in the extreme. I did not have the faintest conception of what that meant except that it was an American way of doing things. Nothing came of it, however, and during the next few months I had to travel from one to another place in France and Germany to cure the ills of the power plants. On my return to Paris I submitted to one of the administrators of the Company, Mr. Rau, a plan for improving their dynamos and was given an opportunity. My success was complete and the delighted directors accorded me the privilege of developing automatic regulators which were much desired.

Shortly after there was some trouble with the lighting plant which had been installed at the new railroad station in Strassburg, Alsace. The wiring was defective and on the occasion of the opening ceremonies a large part of a wall was blown out thru a short-circuit right in the presence of old Emperor William I. The German Government refused to take the plant and the French Company was facing a serious loss. On account of my knowledge of the German language and past experience, I was entrusted with the difficult task of straightening out matters and early in 1883 I went to Strassburg on that mission.

Some of the incidents in that city have left an indelible record on my memory. By a curious coincidence, a number of men who subsequently achieved fame, lived there about that time. In later life I used to say, "There were bacteria of greatness in that old town. Others caught the disease but I escaped!" The practical work, correspondence, and conferences with officials kept me preoccupied day and night, but, as soon as I was able to manage I undertook the construction of a simple motor in a mechanical shop opposite the railroad station, having brought with me from Paris some material for that purpose. The consummation of the experiment was, however, delayed until the summer of that year when I finally had the satisfaction of seeing rotation effected by alternating currents of different phase, and without sliding contacts or commutator, as I had conceived a year before. It was an exquisite pleasure but not to compare with the delirium of joy following the first revelation.

Among my new friends was the former Mayor of the city, Mr. Bauzin, whom I had already in a measure acquainted with this and other inventions of mine and whose support I endeavored to enlist.

He was sincerely devoted to me and put my project before several wealthy persons but, to my mortification, found no response. He wanted to help me in every possible way and the approach of the first of July, 1919, happens to remind me of a form of "assistance" I received from that charming man, which was not financial but none the less appreciated. In 1870, when the Germans invaded the country, Mr. Bauzin had buried a good sized allotment of St. Estephe of 1801 and he came to the conclusion that he knew no worthier person than myself to consume that precious beverage. This, I may say, is one of the unforgettable incidents to which I have referred. My friend urged me to return to Paris as soon as possible and seek support there. This I was anxious to do but my work and negotiations were protracted owing to all sorts of petty obstacles I encountered so that at times the situation seemed hopeless.

Just to give an idea of German thoroness and "efficiency", I may mention here a rather funny experience. An incandescent lamp of 16 c.p. was to be placed in a hallway and upon selecting the proper location I ordered the monteur to run the wires. After working for a while he concluded that the engineer had to be consulted and this was done. The latter made several objections but ultimately agreed that the lamp should be placed two inches from the spot I had assigned, whereupon the work proceeded. Then the engineer became worried and told me that Inspector Averdeck should be notified. That important person called, investigated, debated, and decided that the lamp should be shifted back two inches, which was the place I had marked. It was not long, however, before Averdeck got cold feet himself and advised me that he had informed Ober-Inspector Hieronimus of the matter and that I should await his decision. It was several days before the Ober-Inspector was able to free himself of other pressing duties but at last he arrived and a two-hour debate followed, when he decided to move the lamp two inches farther. My hopes that this was the final act were shattered when the Ober-Inspector returned and said to me: "Regierungsrath Funke is so particular that I would not dare to give an order for placing this lamp without his explicit approval." Accordingly arrangements for a visit from that great man were made. We started cleaning up and polishing early in the morning. Everybody brushed up, I put on my gloves and when Funke came with his retinue he was ceremoniously received.

After two hours' deliberation he suddenly exclaimed: "I must be going," and pointing to a place on the ceiling, he ordered me to put the lamp there. It was the exact spot which I had originally chosen.

So it went day after day with variations, but I was determined to achieve at whatever cost and in the end my efforts were rewarded. By the spring of 1884 all the differences were adjusted, the plant formally accepted, and I returned to Paris with pleasing anticipations. One of the administrators had promised me a liberal compensation in case I succeeded, as well as a fair consideration of the improvements I had made in their dynamos and I hoped to realize a substantial sum. There were three administrators whom I shall designate as A, B and C for convenience. When I called on A he told me that B had the say. This gentleman thought that only C could decide and the latter was quite sure that A alone had the power to act. After several laps of this circulus vivios it dawned upon me that my reward was a castle in Spain.

The utter failure of my attempts to raise capital for development was another disappointment and when Mr. Batchellor prest me to go to America with a view of redesigning the Edison machines, I determined to try my fortunes in the Land of Golden Promise.But the chance was nearly mist. I liquefied my modest assets, secured accommodations and found myself at the railroad station as the train was pulling out. At that moment I discovered that my money and tickets were gone. What to do was the question. Hercules had plenty of time to deliberate but I had to decide while running alongside the train with opposite feelings surging in my brain like condenser oscillations. Resolve, helped by dexterity, won out in the nick of time and upon passing thru the usual experiences, as trivial as unpleasant, I managed to embark for New York with the remnants of my belongings, some poems and articles I had written, and a package of calculations relating to solutions of an unsolvable integral and to my flying machine. During the voyage I sat most of the time at the stern of the ship watching for an opportunity to save somebody from a watery grave, without the slightest thought of danger. Later when I had absorbed some of the practical American sense I shivered at the recollection and marvelled at my former folly.

I wish that I could put in words my first impressions of this country. In the Arabian Tales I read how genii transported people into a land of dreams to live thru delightful adventures. My case was just the reverse. The genii had carried me from a world of dreams into one of realities. What I had left was beautiful, artistic and fascinating in every way; what I saw here was machined, rough and unattractive. A burly policeman was twirling his stick which looked to me as big as a log. I approached him politely with the request to direct me. "Six blocks down, then to the left," he said, with murder in his eyes. "Is this America?" I asked myself in painful surprise. "It is a century behind Europe in civilization." When I went abroad in 1889 —five years having elapsed since my arrival here — I became convinced that it was more than one hundred years AHEAD of Europe and nothing has happened to this day to change my opinion.

The meeting with Edison was a memorable event in my life. I was amazed at this wonderful man who, without early advantages and scientific training, had accomplished so much. I had studied a dozen languages, delved in literature and art, and had spent my best years in libraries reading all sorts of stuff that fell into my hands, from Newton's "Principia" to the novels of Paul de Kock, and felt that most of my life had been squandered. But it did not take long before I recognized that it was the best thing I could have done. Within a few weeks I had won Edison's confidence and it came about in this way.

The S.S. Oregon, the fastest passenger steamer at that time, had both of its lighting machines disabled and its sailing was delayed. As the superstructure had been built after their installation it was impossible to remove them from the hold. The predicament was a serious one and Edison was much annoyed. In the evening I took the necessary instruments with me and went aboard the vessel where I stayed for the night. The dynamos were in bad condition, having several short-circuits and breaks, but with the assistance of the crew I succeeded in putting them in good shape. At five o'clock in the morning, when passing along Fifth Avenue on my way to the shop, I met Edison with Batchellor and a few others as they were returning home to retire. "Here is our Parisian running around at night," he said. When I told him that I was coming from the Oregon and had repaired both machines, he looked at me in silence and walked away without another word. But when he had gone some distance I heard him remark: "Batchellor, this is a good man," and from that time on I had full freedom in directing the work. For nearly a year my regular hours were from 10.30 A.M. until 5 o'clock the next morning without a day's exception. Edison said to me: "I have had many hard-working assistants but you take the cake." During this period I designed twenty-four different types of standard machines with short cores and of uniform pattern which replaced the old ones. The Manager had promised me fifty thousand dollars on the completion of this task but it turned out to be a practical joke. This gave me a painful shock and I resigned my position.

Immediately thereafter some people approached me with the proposal of forming an arc light company under my name, to which I agreed. Here finally was an opportunity to develop the motor, but when I broached the subject to my new associates, they said: "No, we want the arc lamp. We don't care for this alternating current of yours." In 1886 my system of arc lighting was perfected and adopted for factory and municipal lighting, and I was free, but with no other possession than a beautifully engraved certificate of stock of hypothetical value. Then followed a period of struggle in the new medium for which I was not fitted, but the reward came in the end and in April, 1887, the Tesla Electric Company was organized, providing a laboratory and facilities. The motors I built there were exactly as I had imagined them. I made no attempt to improve the design, but merely reproduced the pictures as they appeared to my vision and the operation was always as I expected.

In the early part of 1888 an arrangement was made with the Westinghouse Company for the manufacture of the motors on a large scale. But great difficulties had still to be overcome. My system was based on the use of low frequency currents and the Westinghouse experts had adopted 133 cycles with the object of securing advantages in the transformation. They did not want to depart from their standard forms of apparatus and my efforts had to be concentrated upon adapting the motor to these conditions. Another necessity was to produce a motor capable of running efficiently at this frequency on two wires which was not easy of accomplishment.

At the close of 1889, however, my services in Pittsburg being no longer essential, I returned to New York and resumed experimental work in a laboratory on Grand Street, where I began immediately the design of high frequency machines. The problems of construction in this unexplored field were novel and quite peculiar and I encountered many difficulties. I rejected the inductor type, fearing that it might not yield perfect sine waves which were so important to resonant action. Had it not been for this I could have saved myself a great deal of labor. Another discouraging feature of the high frequency alternator seemed to be the inconstancy of speed which threatened to impose serious limitations to its use. I had already noted in my demonstrations before the American Institution of Electrical Engineers that several times the tune was lost, necessitating readjustment, and did not yet foresee, what I discovered long afterwards, a means of operating a machine of this kind at a speed constant to such a degree as not to vary more than a small fraction of one revolution between the extremes of load.

From many other considerations it appeared desirable to invent a simpler device for the production of electric oscillations. In 1856 Lord Kelvin had exposed the theory of the condenser discharge, but no practical application of that important knowledge was made. I saw the possibilities and undertook the development of induction apparatus on this principle. My progress was so rapid as to enable me to exhibit at my lecture in 1891 a coil giving sparks of five inches.

On that occasion I frankly told the engineers of a defect involved in the transformation by the new method, namely, the loss in the spark gap. Subsequent investigation showed that no matter what medium is employed, be it air, hydrogen, mercury vapor, oil or a stream of electrons, the efficiency is the same. It is a law very much like that governing the conversion of mechanical energy. We may drop a weight from a certain height vertically down or carry it to the lower level along any devious path, it is immaterial insofar as the amount of work is concerned. Fortunately however, this drawback is not fatal as by proper proportioning of the resonant circuits an efficiency of 85 per cent is attainable. Since my early announcement of the invention it has come into universal use and wrought a revolution in many departments. But a still greater future awaits it.

When in 1900 I obtained powerful discharges of 100 feet and flashed a current around the globe, I was reminded of the first tiny spark I observed in my Grand Street laboratory and was thrilled by sensations akin to those I felt when I discovered the rotating magnetic field.

V.
The Magnifying Transmitter

As I review the events of my past life I realize how subtle are the influences that shape our destinies. An incident of my youth may serve to illustrate. One winter's day I managed to climb a steep mountain, in company with other boys. The snow was quite deep and a warm southerly wind made it just suitable for our purpose. We amused ourselves by throwing balls which would roll down a certain distance, gathering more or less snow, and we tried to outdo one another in this exciting sport. Suddenly a ball was seen to go beyond the limit, swelling to enormous proportions until it became as big as a house and plunged thundering into the valley below with a force that made the ground tremble. I looked on spellbound, incapable of understanding what had happened. For weeks afterward the picture of the avalanche was before my eyes and I wondered how anything so small could grow to such an immense size. Ever since that time the magnification of feeble actions fascinated me, and when, years later, I took up the experimental study of mechanical and electrical resonance, I was keenly interested from the very start. Possibly, had it not been for that early powerful impression, I might not have followed up the little spark I obtained with my coil and never developed my best invention, the true history of which I'll tell here for the first time.

"Lionhunters" have often asked me which of my discoveries I prize most. This depends on the point of view. Not a few technical men, very able in their special departments, but dominated by a pedantic spirit and nearsighted, have asserted that excepting the induction motor I have given to the world little of practical use. This is a grievous mistake. A new idea must not be judged by its immediate results. My alternating system of power transmission came at a psychological moment, as a long-sought answer to pressing industrial questions, and altho considerable resistance had to be overcome and opposing interests reconciled, as usual, the commercial introduction could not be long delayed. Now, compare this situation with that confronting my turbine, for example. One should think that so simple and beautiful an invention, possessing many features of an ideal motor, should be adopted at once and, undoubtedly, it would under similar conditions. But the prospective effect of the rotating field was not to render worthless existing machinery; on the contrary, it was to give it additional value. The system lent itself to new enterprise as well as to improvement of the old. My turbine is an advance of a character entirely different. It is a radical departure in the sense that its success would mean the abandonment of the antiquated types of prime movers on which billions of dollars have been spent. Under such circumstances the progress must needs be slow and perhaps the greatest impediment is encountered in the prejudicial opinions created in the minds of experts by organized opposition.

Only the other day I had a disheartening experience when I met my friend and former assistant, Charles F. Scott, now professor of Electrical Engineering at Yale. I had not seen him for a long time and was glad to have an opportunity for a little chat at my office. Our conversation naturally enough drifted on my turbine and I became heated to a high degree. "Scott," I exclaimed, carried away by the vision of a glorious future, "my turbine will scrap all the heat–

engines in the world." Scott stroked his chin and looked away thoughtfully, as though making a mental calculation. "That will make quite a pile of scrap," he said, and left without another word!

These and other inventions of mine, however, were nothing more than steps forward in certain directions. In evolving them I simply followed the inborn sense to improve the present devices without any special thought of our far more imperative necessities. The "Magnifying Transmitter" was the product of labors extending through years, having for their chief object the solution of problems which are infinitely more important to mankind than mere industrial development.

If my memory serves me right, it was in November, 1890, that I performed a laboratory experiment which was one of the most extraordinary and spectacular ever recorded in the annals of science. In investigating the behaviour of high frequency currents I had satisfied myself that an electric field of sufficient intensity could be produced in a room to light up electrodeless vacuum tubes. Accordingly, a transformer was built to test the theory and the first trial proved a marvelous success. It is difficult to appreciate what those strange phenomena meant at that time. We crave for new sensations but soon become indifferent to them. The wonders of yesterday are today common occurrences. When my tubes were first publicly exhibited they were viewed with amazement impossible to describe. From all parts of the world I received urgent invitations and numerous honors and other flattering inducements were offered to me, which I declined.

But in 1892 the demands became irresistible and I went to London where I delivered a lecture before the Institution of Electrical Engineers. It had been my intention to leave immediately for Paris in compliance with a similar obligation, but Sir James Dewar insisted on my appearing before the Royal Institution. I was a man of firm resolve but succumbed easily to the forceful arguments of the great Scotsman. He pushed me into a chair and poured out half a glass of a wonderful brown fluid which sparkled in all sorts of iridescent colors and tasted like nectar. "Now," said he. "you are sitting in Faraday's chair and you are enjoying whiskey he used to drink." In both aspects it was an enviable experience. The next evening I gave a demonstration before that Institution, at the termination of which Lord Rayleigh addressed the audience and his generous words gave me the first start in these endeavors. I fled from London and later from Paris to escape favors showered upon me, and journeyed to my home where I passed through a most painful ordeal and illness. Upon regaining my health I began to formulate plans for the resumption of work in America. Up to that time I never realized that I possessed any particular gift of discovery but Lord Rayleigh, whom I always considered as an ideal man of science, had said so and if that was the case I felt that I should concentrate on some big idea.

One day, as I was roaming in the mountains, I sought shelter from an approaching storm. The sky became overhung with heavy clouds but somehow the rain was delayed until, all of a sudden, there was a lightning flash and a few moments after a deluge. This observation set me thinking. It was manifest that the two phenomena were closely related, as cause and effect, and a little reflection led me to the conclusion that the electrical energy involved in the precipitation of the water was inconsiderable, the function of lightning being much like that of a sensitive trigger.

Here was a stupendous possibility of achievement. If we could produce electric effects of the required quality, this whole planet and the conditions of existence on it could be transformed. The sun raises the water of the oceans and winds drive it to distant regions where it remains in a state of most delicate balance. If it were in our power to upset it when and wherever desired, this mighty life-sustaining stream could be at will controlled. We could irrigate arid deserts, create lakes and rivers and provide motive power in unlimited amounts. This would be the most efficient way of harnessing the sun to the uses of man. The consummation depended on our ability to develop electric forces of the order of those in nature. It seemed a hopeless undertaking, but I made up my mind to try it and immediately on my return to the United States, in the Summer of 1892, work was begun which was to me all the more attractive, because a means of the same kind was necessary for the successful transmission of energy without wires.

The first gratifying result was obtained in the spring of the succeeding year when I reached tensions of about 1,000,000 volts with my conical coil. That was not much in the light of the present art, but it was then considered a feat. Steady progress was made until the destruction of my laboratory by fire in 1895, as may be judged from an article by T. C. Martin which appeared in the April number of the Century Magazine. This calamity set me back in many ways and most of that year had to be devoted to planning and reconstruction. However, as soon as circumstances permitted, I returned to the task.

Although I knew that higher electro-motive forces were attainable with apparatus of larger dimensions, I had an instinctive perception that the object could be accomplished by the proper design of a comparatively small and compact transformer. In carrying on tests with a secondary in the form of a flat spiral, as illustrated in my patents, the absence of streamers surprised me, and it was not long before I discovered that this was due to the position of the turns and their mutual action. Profiting from this observation I resorted to the use of a high tension conductor with turns of considerable diameter sufficiently separated to keep down the distributed capacity, while at the same time preventing undue accumulation of the charge at any point. The application of this principle enabled me to produce pressures of 4,000,000 volts, which was about the limit obtainable in my new laboratory at Houston Street, as the discharges extended through a distance of 16 feet. A photograph of this transmitter was published in the *Electrical Review* of November, 1898.

In order to advance further along this line I had to go into the open, and in the spring of 1899, having completed preparations for the erection of a wireless plant, I went to Colorado where I remained for more than one year. Here I introduced other improvements and refinements which made it possible to generate currents of any tension that may be desired. Those who are interested will find some information in regard to the experiments I conducted there in my article, "The Problem of Increasing Human Energy" in the *Century Magazine* of June, 1900, to which I have referred on a previous occasion.

I have been asked by the *ELECTRICAL EXPERIMENTER* to be quite explicit on this subject so that my young friends among the readers of the magazine will clearly understand the construction and operation of my "Magnifying Transmitter" and the purposes for which it is intended. Well, then, in the first place, it is a resonant transformer with a secondary in which the parts, charged to a high potential, are of considerable area and arranged in space along ideal enveloping surfaces of very large radii of curvature, and at proper distances from one another thereby insuring a small electric surface density everywhere so that no leak can occur even if the conductor is bare. It is suitable for any frequency, from a few to many thousands of cycles per second, and can be used in the production of currents of tremendous volume and moderate pressure, or of smaller amperage and immense electromotive force. The maximum electric tension is merely dependent on the curvature of the surfaces on which the charged elements are situated and the area of the latter.

Judging from my past experience, as much as 100,000,000 volts are perfectly practicable. On the other hand currents of many thousands of amperes may be obtained in the antenna. A plant of but very moderate dimensions is required for such performances. Theoretically, a terminal of less than 90 feet in diameter is sufficient to develop an electromotive force of that magnitude while for antenna currents of from 2,000–4,000 amperes at the usual frequencies it need not be larger than 30 feet in diameter.

In a more restricted meaning this wireless transmitter is one in which the Hertz-wave radiation is an entirely negligible quantity as compared with the whole energy, under which condition the damping factor is extremely small and an enormous charge is stored in the elevated capacity. Such a circuit may then be excited with impulses of any kind, even of low frequency and it will yield sinusoidal and continuous oscillations like those of an alternator.

Taken in the narrowest significance of the term, however, it is a resonant transformer which, besides possessing these qualities, is accurately proportioned to fit the globe and its electrical constants and properties, by virtue of which design it becomes highly efficient and effective in the wireless transmission of energy. Distance is then absolutely eliminated, there being no diminution in the intensity of the transmitted impulses. It is even possible to make the actions increase with the distance from the plant according to an exact mathematical law.

This invention was one of a number comprised in my "World–System" of wireless transmission which I undertook to commercialize on my return to New York in 1900. As to the immediate purposes of my enterprise, they were clearly outlined in a technical statement of that period from which I quote:

"The 'World-System' has resulted from a combination of several original discoveries made by the inventor in the course of long continued research and experimentation. It makes possible not only the instantaneous and precise wireless transmission of any kind of signals, messages or characters, to all parts of the world, but also the inter-connection of the existing telegraph, telephone, and other signal stations without any change in their present equipment. By its means, for instance, a telephone subscriber here may call up and talk to any other subscriber on the Globe. An inexpensive receiver, not bigger than a watch, will enable him to listen anywhere, on land or sea, to a speech delivered or music played in some other place, however distant. These examples are cited merely to give an idea of the possibilities of this great scientific advance, which annihilates distance and makes that perfect natural conductor, the Earth, available for all the innumerable purposes which human ingenuity has found for a line-wire. One far-reaching result of this is that any device capable of being operated thru one or more wires (at a distance obviously restricted) can likewise be actuated, without artificial conductors and with the same facility and accuracy, at distances to which there are no limits other than those imposed by the physical dimensions of the Globe. Thus, not only will entirely new fields for commercial exploitation be opened up by this ideal method of transmission but the old ones vastly extended."

The "World-System" is based on the application of the following important inventions and discoveries:

1.

The "Tesla Transformer". This apparatus is in the production of electrical vibrations as revolutionary as gunpowder was in warfare. Currents many times stronger than any ever generated in the usual ways, and sparks over one hundred feet long, have been produced by the inventor with an instrument of this kind.

2.

The "Magnifying Transmitter". This is Tesla's best invention, a peculiar transformer specially adapted to excite the Earth, which is in the transmission of electrical energy what the telescope is in astronomical observation. By the use of this marvelous device he has already set up electrical movements of greater intensity than those of lightning and passed a current, sufficient to light more than two hundred incandescent lamps, around the Globe.

3.

The "Tesla Wireless System". This system comprises a number of improvements and is the only means known for transmitting economically electrical energy to a distance without wires. Careful tests and measurements in connection with an experimental station of great activity, erected by the inventor in Colorado, have demonstrated that power in any desired amount can be conveyed, clear across the Globe if necessary, with a loss not exceeding a few per cent.

4.

The "Art of Individualization". This invention of Tesla's is to primitive "tuning" what refined language is to unarticulated expression. It makes possible the transmission of signals or messages absolutely secret and exclusive both in the active and passive aspect, that is, non-interfering as well as non-interferable. Each signal is like an individual of unmistakable identity and there is virtually no limit to the number of stations or instruments which can be simultaneously operated without the slightest mutual disturbance.

5.

The "Terrestrial Stationary Waves". This wonderful discovery, popularly explained, means that the Earth is responsive to electrical vibrations of definite pitch just as a tuning fork to certain waves of sound. These particular electrical vibrations, capable of powerfully exciting the Globe, lend themselves to innumerable uses of great importance commercially and in many other respects.

The first "World-System" power plant can be put in operation in nine months. With this power plant it will be practicable to attain electrical activities up to ten million horsepower and it is designed to serve for as many technical achievements as are possible without due expense. Among these the following may be mentioned:

(1) The inter-connection of the existing telegraph exchanges or offices all over the world;

(2) The establishment of a secret and non-interferable

government telegraph service;

(3) The inter-connection of all the present telephone exchanges or offices on the Globe;

(4) The universal distribution of general news, by telegraph or telephone, in connection with the Press;

(5) The establishment of such a 'World-System' of intelligence transmission for exclusive private use;

(6) The inter-connection and operation of all stock tickers of the world;

(7) The establishment of a 'World-System' of musical distribution, etc.;

(8) The universal registration of time by cheap clocks indicating the hour with astronomical precision and requiring no attention whatever;

(9) The world transmission of typed or handwritten characters, letters, checks, etc.;

(10) The establishment of a universal marine service enabling the navigators of all ships to steer perfectly without compass, to determine the exact location, hour and speed, to prevent collisions and disasters, etc.;

(11) The inauguration of a system of world-printing on land and sea;

(12) The world reproduction of photographic pictures and all kinds of drawings or records.

I also proposed to make demonstrations in the wireless transmission of power on a small scale but sufficient to carry conviction. Besides these I referred to other and incomparably more important applications of my discoveries which will be disclosed at some future date.

A plant was built on Long Island with a tower 187 feet high, having a spherical terminal about 68 feet in diameter. These dimensions were adequate for the transmission of virtually any amount of energy. Originally only from 200 to 300 K.W. were provided but I intended to employ later several thousand horsepower. The transmitter was to emit a wave complex of special characteristics and I had devised a unique method of telephonic control of any amount of energy.

The tower was destroyed two years ago but my projects are

being developed and another one, improved in some features, will be constructed. On this occasion I would contradict the widely circulated report that the structure was demolished by the Government which owing to war conditions, might have created prejudice in the minds of those who may not know that the papers, which thirty years ago conferred upon me the honor of American citizenship, are always kept in a safe, while my orders, diplomas, degrees, gold medals and other distinctions are packed away in old trunks. If this report had a foundation I would have been refunded a large sum of money which I expended in the construction of the tower. On the contrary it was in the interest of the Government to preserve it, particularly as it would have made possible—to mention just one valuable result—the location of a submarine in any part of the world. My plant, services, and all my improvements have always been at the disposal of the officials and ever since the outbreak of the European conflict I have been working at a sacrifice on several inventions of mine relating to aerial navigation, ship propulsion and wireless transmission which are of the greatest importance to the country. Those who are well informed know that my ideas have revolutionized the industries of the

United States and I am not aware that there lives an inventor who has been, in this respect, as fortunate as myself especially as regards the use of his improvements in the war. I have refrained from publicly expressing myself on this subject before as it seemed improper to dwell on personal matters while all the world was in dire trouble.

I would add further, in view of various rumors which have reached me, that Mr. J. Pierpont Morgan did not interest himself with me in a business way but in the same large spirit in which he has assisted many other pioneers. He carried out his generous promise to the letter and it would have been most unreasonable to expect from him anything more. He had the highest regard for my attainments and gave me every evidence of his complete faith in my ability to ultimately achieve what I had set out to do. I am unwilling to accord to some smallminded and jealous individuals the satisfaction of having thwarted my efforts. These men are to me nothing more than microbes of a nasty disease. My project was retarded by laws of nature. The world was not prepared for it. It was too far ahead of time. But the same laws will prevail in the end and make it a triumphal success.

VI.
The Art of Telautomatics

No subject to which I have ever devoted myself has called for such concentration of mind and strained to so dangerous a degree the finest fibers of my brain as the system of which the Magnifying Transmitter is the foundation. I put all the intensity and vigor of youth in the development of the rotating field discoveries, but those early labors were of a different character. Although strenuous in the extreme, they did not involve that keen and exhausting discernment which had to be exercised in attacking the many puzzling problems of the wireless. Despite my rare physical endurance at that period the abused nerves finally rebelled and I suffered a complete collapse, just as the consummation of the long and difficult task was almost in sight.

Without doubt I would have paid a greater penalty later, and very likely my career would have been prematurely terminated, had not providence equipt me with a safety device, which has seemed to improve with advancing years and unfailingly comes into play when my forces are at an end. So long as it operates I am safe from danger, due to overwork, which threatens other inventors and, incidentally, I need no vacations which are indispensable to most people. When I am all but used up I simply do as the darkies, who "naturally fall asleep while white folks worry." To venture a theory out of my sphere, the body probably accumulates little by little a definite quantity of some toxic agent and I sink into a nearly lethargic state which lasts half an hour to the minute. Upon awakening I have the sensation as though the events immediately preceding had occurred very long ago, and if I attempt to continue the interrupted train of thought I feel a veritable mental nausea. Involuntarily I then turn to other work and am surprised at the freshness of the mind and ease with which I overcome obstacles that had baffled me before. After weeks or months my passion for the temporarily abandoned invention returns and I invariably find answers to all the vexing questions with scarcely any effort. In this connection I will tell of an extraordinary experience which may be of interest to students of psychology.

I had produced a striking phenomenon with my grounded transmitter and was endeavoring to ascertain its true significance in relation to the currents propagated through the earth. It seemed a hopeless undertaking, and for more than a year I worked unremittingly, but in vain. This profound study so entirely absorbed me that I became forgetful of everything else, even of my undermined health. At last, as I was at the point of breaking down, nature applied the preservative inducing lethal sleep. Regaining my senses I realized with consternation that I was unable to visualize scenes from my life except those of infancy, the very first ones that had entered my consciousness. Curiously enough, these appeared before my vision with startling distinctness and afforded me welcome relief. Night after night, when retiring, I would think of them and more and more of my previous existence was revealed. The image of my mother was always the principal figure in the spectacle that slowly unfolded, and a consuming desire to see her again gradually took possession of me. This feeling grew so strong that I resolved to drop all work and satisfy my longing. But I found it too hard to break away from the laboratory, and several months elapsed during which I had succeeded in reviving all the impressions of my past life up to the spring of 1892. In the next picture that came out of the mist of oblivion, I saw myself at the Hotel de la Paix in Paris just coming to from one of my peculiar sleeping spells, which had been caused by prolonged exertion of the brain. Imagine the pain and distress I felt when it flashed upon my mind that a dispatch was handed to me at that very moment bearing the sad news that my mother was dying. I remembered how I made the long journey home without an hour of rest and how she passed away after weeks of agony! It was especially remarkable that during all this period of partially obliterated memory I was fully alive to everything touching on the subject of my research. I could recall the smallest details and the least significant observations in my experiments and even recite pages of text and complex mathematical formulae.

My belief is firm in a law of compensation. The true rewards are ever in proportion to the labor and sacrifices made. This is one of the reasons why I feel certain that of all my inventions, the Magnifying Transmitter will prove most important and valuable to future generations. I am prompted to this prediction not so much by thoughts of the commercial and industrial revolution which it will surely bring about, but of the humanitarian consequences of the many achievements it makes possible. Considerations of mere utility weigh little in the balance against the higher benefits of civilization. We are confronted with portentous problems which can not be solved just by providing for our material existence, however abundantly. On the contrary, progress in this direction is fraught with hazards and perils not less menacing than those born from want and suffering. If we were to release the energy of atoms or discover some other way of developing cheap and unlimited power at any point of the globe this accomplishment, instead of being a blessing, might bring disaster to mankind in giving rise to dissension and anarchy which would ultimately result in the enthronement of the hated regime of force. The greatest good will comes from technical improvements tending to unification and harmony, and my wireless transmitter is preeminently such. By its means the human voice and likeness will be reproduced everywhere and factories driven thousands of miles from waterfalls furnishing the power; aerial machines will be propelled around the earth without a stop and the sun's energy controlled to create lakes and rivers for motive purposes and transformation of arid deserts into fertile land. Its introduction for telegraphic, telephonic and similar uses will automatically cut out the statics and all other interferences which at present impose narrow limits to the application of the wireless.

This is a timely topic on which a few words might not be amiss. During the past decade a number of people have arrogantly claimed that they had succeeded in doing away with this impediment. I have carefully examined all of the arrangements described and tested most of them long before they were publicly disclosed, but the finding was uniformly negative. A recent official statement from the U.S. Navy may, perhaps, have taught some beguilable news editors how to appraise these announcments at their real worth. As a rule the attempts are based on theories so fallacious that whenever they come to my notice I can not help thinking in a lighter vein. Quite recently a new discovery was heralded, with a deafening flourish of trumpets, but it proved another case of a mountain bringing forth a mouse.

This reminds me of an exciting incident which took place years ago when I was conducting my experiments with currents of high frequency. Steve Brodie had just jumped off the Brooklyn Bridge. The feat has been vulgarized since by imitators, but the first report electrified New York. I was very impressionable then and frequently spoke of the daring printer. On a hot afternoon I felt the necessity of refreshing myself and stepped into one of the popular thirty thousand institutions of this great city where a delicious twelve per cent beverage was served which can now be had only by making a trip to the poor and devastated countries of Europe. The attendance was large and not over distinguished and a matter was discussed which gave me an admirable opening for the careless remark: "This is what I said when I jumped off the bridge." No sooner had I uttered these words than I felt like the companion of Timotheus in the poem of Schiller. In an instant there was a pandemonium and a dozen voices cried: "It is Brodie!" I threw a quarter on the counter and bolted for the door but the crowd was at my heels with yells: "Stop, Steve!" which must have been misunderstood for many persons tried to hold me up as I ran frantically for my haven of refuge. By darting around corners I fortunately managed – through the medium of a fire–escape – to reach the laboratory where I threw off my coat, camouflaged myself as a hard-working blacksmith, and started the forge. But these precautions proved unnecessary; I had eluded my pursuers. For many years afterward, at night, when imagination turns into spectres the trifling troubles of the day, I often thought, as I tossed on the bed, what my fate would have been had that mob caught me and found out that I was not Steve Brodie!

Now the engineer, who lately gave an account before a technical body of a novel remedy against statics based on a "heretofore unknown law of nature", seems to have been as reckless as myself when he contended that these disturbances propagate up and down, while those of a transmitter proceed along the earth. It would mean that a condenser, as this globe, with its gaseous envelope, could be charged and discharged in a manner quite contrary to the fundamental teachings propounded in every elemental text-book of physics. Such a supposition would have been condemned as erroneous, even in Franklin's time, for the facts bearing on this were then well known and the identity between atmospheric electricity and that developed by machines was fully established. Obviously, natural and artificial disturbances propagate through the earth and the air in exactly the same way, and both set up electromotive forces in the horizontal, as well as vertical, sense. Interference can not be overcome by any such methods as were proposed. The truth is this: in the air the potential increases at the rate of about fifty volts per foot of elevation, owing to which there may be a difference of pressure amounting to twenty, or even forty thousand volts between the upper and lower ends of the antenna. The masses of the charged atmosphere are constantly in motion and give up electricity to the conductor, not continuously but rather disruptively, this producing a grinding noise in a sensitive telephonic receiver. The higher the terminal and the greater the space encompassed by the wires, the more pronounced is the effect, but it must be understood that it is purely local and has little to do with the real trouble.

In 1900, while perfecting my wireless system, one form of apparatus comprised four antennae. These were carefully calibrated to the same frequency and connected in multiple with the object of magnifying the action, in receiving from any direction. When I desired to ascertain the origin of the transmitted impulses, each diagonally situated pair was put in series with a primary coil energizing the detector circuit. In the former case the sound was loud in the telephone; in the latter it ceased, as expected, the two antennae neutralizing each other, but the true statics manifested themselves in both instances and I had to devise special preventives embodying different principles.

By employing receivers connected to two points of the ground, as suggested by me long ago, this trouble caused by the charged air, which is very serious in the structures as now built, is nullified and besides, the liability of all kinds of interference is reduced to about one-half, because of the directional character of the circuit. This was perfectly self-evident, but came as a revelation to some simple-minded wireless folks whose experience was confined to forms of apparatus that could have been improved with an axe, and they have been disposing of the bear's skin before killing him. If it were true that strays performed such antics, it would be easy to get rid of them by receiving without aerials. But, as a matter of fact, a wire buried in the ground which, conforming to this view, should be absolutely immune, is more susceptible to certain extraneous impulses than one placed vertically in the air. To state it fairly, a slight progress has been made, but not by virtue of any particular method or device. It was achieved simply by discarding the enormous structures, which are bad enough for transmission but wholly unsuitable for reception, and adopting a more appropriate type of receiver. As I pointed out in a previous article, to dispose of this difficulty for good, a radical change must be made in the system, and the sooner this is done the better.

It would be calamitous, indeed, if at this time when the art is in its infancy and the vast majority, not excepting even experts, have no conception of its ultimate possibilities, a measure would be rushed through the legislature making it a government monopoly. This was proposed a few weeks ago by Secretary Daniels, and no doubt that distinguished official has made his appeal to the Senate and House of Representatives with sincere conviction. But universal evidence unmistakably shows that the best results are always obtained in healthful commercial competition. There are, however, exceptional reasons why wireless should be given the fullest freedom of development. In the first place it offers prospects immeasurably greater and more vital to betterment of human life than any other invention or discovery in the history of man. Then again, it must be understood that this wonderful art has been, in its entirety, evolved here and can be called "American" with more right and propriety than the telephone, the incandescent lamp or the aeroplane. Enterprising press agents and stock jobbers have been so successful in spreading misinformation that even so excellent a periodical as the *Scientific American* accords the chief credit to a foreign country. The Germans, of course, gave us the Hertz-waves and the Russian, English, French and Italian experts were quick in using them for signaling purposes. It was an obvious application of the new agent and accomplished with the old classical and unimproved induction coil – scarcely anything more than another kind of heliography. The radius of transmission was very limited, the results attained of little value, and the Hertz oscillations, as a means for conveying intelligence, could have been advantageously replaced by sound-waves, which I advocated in 1891. Moreover, all of these attempts were made three years after the basic principles of the wireless system, which is universally employed to-day, and its potent instrumentalities had been clearly described and developed in America. No trace of those Hertzian appliances and methods remains today. We have proceeded in the very opposite direction and what has been done is the product of the brains and efforts of citizens of this country. The fundamental patents have expired and the opportunities are open to all. The chief argument of the Secretary is based on interference. According to his statement, reported in *the New York Herald* of July 29th, signals from a powerful station can be intercepted in every village of the world . In view of this fact, which was demonstrated in my experiments of 1900, it would be of little use to impose restrictions in the United States.

As throwing light on this point, I may mention that only recently an odd looking gentleman called on me with the object of enlisting my services in the construction of world transmitters in some distant land.

"We have no money," he said, "but carloads of solid gold and we will give you a liberal amount." I told him that I wanted to see first what will be done with my inventions in America, and this ended the interview. But I am satisfied that some dark forces are at work, and as time goes on the maintenance of continuous communication will be rendered more difficult. The only remedy is a system immune against interruption. It has been perfected, it exists, and all that is necessary is to put it in operation.

The terrible conflict is still uppermost in the minds and perhaps the greatest importance will be attached to the Magnifying Transmitter as a machine for attack and defense, more particularly in connection with Telautomatics. This invention is a logical outcome of observations begun in my boyhood and continued thruout my life. When the first results were published *the Electrical Review* stated editorially that it would become one of the "most potent factors in the advance and civilization of mankind". The time is not distant when this prediction will be fulfilled. In 1898 and 1900 it was offered to the Government and might have been adopted were I one of those who would go to Alexander's shepherd when they want a favor from Alexander. At that time I really thought that it would abolish war, because of its unlimited destructiveness and exclusion of the personal element of combat. But while I have not lost faith in its potentialities, my views have changed since.

War can not be avoided until the physical cause for its recurrence is removed and this, in the last analysis, is the vast extent of the planet on which we live. Only thru annihilation of distance in every respect, as the conveyance of intelligence, transport of passengers and supplies and transmission of energy will conditions be brought about some day, insuring permanency of friendly relations. What we now want most is closer contact and better understanding between individuals and communities all over the earth, and the elimination of that fanatic devotion to exalted ideals of national egoism and pride which is always prone to plunge the world into primeval barbarism and strife. No league or parliamentary act of any kind will ever prevent such a calamity. These are only new devices for putting the weak at the mercy of the strong.

I have expressed myself in this regard fourteen years ago, when a combination of a few leading governments – a sort of Holy Alliance – was advocated by the late Andrew Carnegie, who may be fairly considered as the father of this idea, having given to it more publicity and impetus than anybody else prior to the efforts of the President. While it can not be denied that such a pact might be of material advantage to some less fortunate peoples, it can not attain the chief object sought. Peace can only come as a natural consequence of universal enlightenment and merging of races, and we are still far from this blissful realization.

As I view the world of today, in the light of the gigantic struggle we have witnessed, I am filled with conviction that the interests of humanity would be best served if the United States remained true to its traditions and kept out of "entangling alliances." Situated as it is, geographically, remote from the theaters of impending conflicts, without incentive to territorial aggrandizement, with inexhaustible resources and immense population thoroly imbued with the spirit of liberty and right, this country is placed in a unique and privileged position. It is thus able to exert, independently, its colossal strength and moral force to the benefit of all, more judiciously and effectively, than as member of a league.

In one of these biographical sketches, published in the *ELECTRICAL EXPERIMENTER*, I have dwelt on the circumstances of my early life and told of an affliction which compelled me to unremitting exercise of imagination and self observation. This mental activity, at first involuntary under the pressure of illness and suffering, gradually became second nature and led me finally to recognize that I was but an automaton devoid of free will in thought and action and merely responsive to the forces of the environment. Our bodies are of such complexity of structure, the motions we perform are so numerous and involved, and the external impressions on our sense organs to such a degree delicate and elusive that it is hard for the average person to grasp this fact. And yet nothing is more convincing to the trained investigator than the mechanistic theory of life which had been, in a measure, understood and propounded by Descartes three hundred years ago. But in his time many important functions of our organism were unknown and, especially with respect to the nature of light and the construction and operation of the eye, philosophers were in the dark.

In recent years the progress of scientific research in these fields has been such as to leave no room for a doubt in regard to this view on which many works have been published. One of its ablest and most eloquent exponents is, perhaps, Felix Le Dantec, formerly assistant of Pasteur. Prof. Jacques Loeb has performed remarkable experiments in heliotropism, clearly establishing the controlling power of light in lower forms of organisms, and his latest book, *Forced Movements*, is revelatory. But while men of science accept this theory simply as any other that is recognized, to me it is a truth which I hourly demonstrate by every act and thought of mine. The consciousness of the external impression prompting me to any kind of exertion, physical or mental, is ever present in my mind. Only on very rare occasions, when I was in a state of exceptional concentration, have I found difficulty in locating the original impulses.

The by far greater number of human beings are never aware of what is passing around and within them, and millions fall victims of disease and die prematurely just on this account. The commonest every-day occurrences appear to them mysterious and inexplicable. One may feel a sudden wave of sadness and rake his brain for an explanation when he might have noticed that it was caused by a cloud cutting off the rays of the sun. He may see the image of a friend dear to him under conditions which he construes as very peculiar, when only shortly before he has passed him in the street or seen his photograph somewhere. When he loses a collar button he fusses and swears for an hour, being unable to visualize his previous actions and locate the object directly. Deficient observation is merely a form of ignorance and responsible for the many morbid notions and foolish ideas prevailing. There is not more than one out of every ten persons who does not believe in telepathy and other psychic manifestations, spiritualism and communion with the dead, and who would refuse to listen to willing or unwilling deceivers.

Just to illustrate how deeply rooted this tendency has become even among the clearheaded American population, I may mention a comical incident. Shortly before the war, when the exhibition of my turbines in this city elicited widespread comment in the technical papers, I anticipated that there would. be a scramble among manufacturers to get hold of the invention, and I had particular designs on that man from Detroit who has an uncanny faculty for accumulating millions. So confident was I that he would turn up some day, that I declared this as certain to my secretary and assistants. Sure enough, one fine morning a body of engineers from the Ford Motor Company presented themselves with the request of discussing with me an important project. "Didn't I tell you?" I remarked triumphantly to my employees, and one of them said, "You are amazing, Mr. Tesla; everything comes out exactly as you predict." As soon as these hard-headed men were seated I, of course, immediately began to extol the wonderful features of my turbine, when the spokesmen interrupted me and said, "We know all about this, but we are on a special errand. We have formed a psychological society for the investigation of psychic phenomena and we want you to join us in this undertaking." I suppose those engineers never knew how near they came to being fired out of my office.

Ever since I was told by some of the greatest men of the time, leaders in science whose names are immortal, that I am possesst of an unusual mind, I bent all my thinking faculties on the solution of great problems regardless of sacrifice. For many years I endeavored to solve the enigma of death, and watched eagerly for every kind of spiritual indication. But only once in the course of my existence have I had an experience which momentarily impressed me as supernatural. It was at the time of my mother's death.

I had become completely exhausted by pain and long vigilance, and one night was carried to a building about two blocks from our home. As I lay helpless there, I thought that if my mother died while I was away from her bedside she would surely give me a sign. Two or three months before I was in London in company with my late friend, Sir William Crookes, when spiritualism was discussed, and

I was under the full sway of these thoughts. I might not have paid attention to other men, but was susceptible to his arguments as it was his epochal work on radiant matter, which I had read as a student, that made me embrace the electrical career. I reflected that the conditions for a look into the beyond were most favorable, for my mother was a woman of genius and particularly excelling in the powers of intuition. During the whole night every fiber in my brain was strained in expectancy, but nothing happened until early in the morning, when I fell in a sleep, or perhaps a swoon, and saw a cloud carrying angelic figures of marvelous beauty, one of whom gazed upon me lovingly and gradually assumed the features of my mother. The appearance slowly floated across the room and vanished, and I was awakened by an indescribably sweet song of many voices.In that instant a certitude, which no words can express, came upon me that my mother had just died. And that was true. I was unable to understand the tremendous weight of the painful knowledge I received in advance, and wrote a letter to Sir William Crookes while still under the domination of these impressions and in poor bodily health.

When I recovered I sought for a long time the external cause of this strange manifestation and, to my great relief, I succeeded after many months of fruitless effort. I had seen the painting of a celebrated artist, representing allegorically one of the seasons in the form of a cloud with a group of angels which seemed to actually float in the air, and this had struck me forcefully. It was exactly the same that appeared in my dream, with the exception of my mother's likeness. The music came from the choir in the church nearby at the early mass of Easter morning, explaining everything satisfactorily in conformity with scientific facts.

This occurred long ago, and I have never had the faintest reason since to change my views on psychical and spiritual phenomena, for which there is absolutely no foundation. The belief in these is the natural outgrowth of intellectual development. Religious dogmas are no longer accepted in their orthodox meaning, but every individual clings to faith in a supreme power of some kind. We all must have an ideal to govern our conduct and insure contentment, but it is immaterial whether it be one of creed, art, science or anything else, so long as it fulfills the function of a dematerializing force. It is essential to the peaceful existence of humanity as a whole that one common conception should prevail.

While I have failed to obtain any evidence in support of the contentions of psychologists and spiritualists, I have proved to my complete satisfaction the automatism of life, not only through continuous observations of individual actions, but even more conclusively through certain generalizations. These amount to a discovery which I consider of the greatest moment to human society, and on which I shall briefly dwell. I got the first inkling of this astounding truth when I was still a very young man, but for many years I int erpreted what I noted simply as coincidences. Namely, whenever either myself or a person to whom I was attached, or a cause to which I was devoted, was hurt by others in a particular way, which might be best popularly characterized as the most unfair imaginable, I experienced a singular and undefinable pain which, for want of a better term, I have qualified as "cosmic", and shortly thereafter, and invariably, those who had inflicted it came to grief. After many such cases I confided this to a number of friends, who had the opportunity to convince themselves of the truth of the theory which I have gradually formulated and which may be stated in the following few words:

Our bodies are of similar construction and exposed to the same external influences. This results in likeness of response and concordance of the general activities on which all our social and other rules and laws are based. We are automata entirely controlled by the forces of the medium being tossed about like corks on the surface of the water, but mistaking the resultant of the impulses from the outside for free will. The movements and other actions we perform are always life preservative and tho seemingly quite independent from one another, we are connected by invisible links. So long as the organism is in perfect order it responds accurately to the agents that prompt it, but the moment that there is some derangement in any individual, his self–preservative power is impaired.

Everybody understands, of course, that if one becomes deaf, has his eyesight weakened, or his limbs injured, the chances for his continued existence are lessened. But this is also true, and perhaps more so, of certain defects in the brain which deprive the automaton, more or less, of that vital quality and cause it to rush into destruction. A very sensitive and observant being, with his highly developed mechanism all intact, and acting with precision in obedience to the changing conditions of the environment, is endowed with a transcending mechanical sense, enabling him to evade perils too subtle to be directly perceived. When he comes in contact with others whose controlling organs are radically faulty, that sense asserts itself and he feels the "cosmic" pain. The truth of this has been borne out in hundreds of instances and I am inviting other students of nature to devote attention to this subject, believing that thru combined and systematic effort results of incalculable value to the world will be attained.

The idea of constructing an automaton, to bear out my theory, presented itself to me early but I did not begin active work until 1893, when I started my wireless investigations. During the succeeding two or three years a number of automatic mechanisms, to be actuated from a distance, were constructed by me and exhibited to visitors in my laboratory.In 1896, however, I designed a complete machine capable of a multitude of operations, but the consummation of my labors was delayed until late in 1897. This machine was illustrated and described in my article in the *Century Magazine* of June, 1900, and other periodicals of that time and, when first shown in the beginning of 1898, it created a sensation such as no other invention of mine has ever produced. In November, 1898, a basic patent on the novel art was granted to me, but only after the Examiner–in–Chief had come to New York and witnessed the performance, for what I claimed seemed unbelievable. I remember that when later I called on an official in Washington, with a view of offering the invention to the Government, he burst out in laughter upon my telling him what I had accomplished. Nobody thought then that there was the faintest prospect of perfecting such a device. It is unfortunate that in this patent, following the advice of my attorneys, I indicated the control as being effected thru the medium of a single circuit and a well–known form of detector, for the reason that I had not yet secured protection on my methods and apparatus for individualization. As a matter of fact, my boats were controlled thru the joint action of several circuits and interference of every kind was excluded. Most generally I employed receiving circuits in the form of loops, including condensers, because the discharges of my high–tension transmitter ionized the air in the hall so that even a very small aerial would draw electricity from the surrounding atmosphere for hours.

Just to give an idea, I found, for instance, that a bulb 12" in diameter, highly exhausted, and with one single terminal to which a short wire was attached, would deliver well on to one thousand successive flashes before all charge of the air in the laboratory was neutralized. The loop form of receiver was not sensitive to such a disturbance and it is curious to note that it is becoming popular at this late date.In reality it collects much less energy than the aerials or a long grounded wire, but it so happens that it does away with a number of defects inherent to the present wireless devices. In demonstrating my invention before audiences, the visitors were requested to ask any questions, however involved, and the automaton would answer them by signs. This was considered magic at that time but was extremely simple, for it was myself who gave the replies by means of the device.

At the same period another larger telautomatic boat was constructed a photograph of which is shown in this number of the *ELECTRICAL EXPERIMENTER*. It was controlled by loops, having several turns placed in the hull, which was made entirely water–tight and capable of submergence. The apparatus was similar to that used in the first with the exception of certain special features I introduced as, for example, incandescent lamps which afforded a visible evidence of the proper functioning of the machine.

These automata, controlled within the range of vision of the operator, were, however, the first and rather crude steps in the evolution of the Art of Telautomatics as I had conceived it. The next logical improvement was its application to automatic mechanisms beyond the limits of vision and at great distance from the center of control, and I have ever since advocated their employment as instruments of warfare in preference to guns. The importance of this now seems to be recognized, if I am to judge from casual announcements thru the press of achievements which are said to be extraordinary but contain no merit of novelty, whatever. In an imperfect manner it is practicable, with the existing wireless plants, to launch an aeroplane, have it follow a certain approximate course, and perform some operation at a distance of many hundreds of miles. A machine of this kind can also be mechanically controlled in several ways and I have no doubt that it may prove of some usefulness in war. But there are, to my best knowledge, no instrumentalities in existence today with which such an object could be accomplished in a precise manner. I have devoted years of study to this matter and have evolved means, making such and greater wonders easily realizable.

As stated on a previous occasion, when I was a student at college I conceived a flying machine quite unlike the present ones. The underlying principle was sound but could not be carried into practice for want of a prime-mover of sufficiently great activity. In recent years I have successfully solved this problem and am now planning aerial machines devoid of sustaining planes, ailerons, propellers and other external attachments, which will be capable of immense speeds and are very likely to furnish powerful arguments for peace in the near future. Such a machine, sustained and propelled entirely by reaction, is shown on page 108 and is supposed to be controlled either mechanically or by wireless energy. By installing proper plants it will be practicable to project a missile of this kind into the air and drop it almost on the very spot designated, which may be thousands of miles away.

But we are not going to stop at this. Telautomata will be ultimately produced, capable of acting as if possest of their own intelligence, and their advent will create a revolution. As early as 1898 I proposed to representatives of a large manufacturing concern the construction and public exhibition of an automobile carriage which, left to itself, would perform a great variety of operations involving something akin to judgment. But my proposal was deemed chimerical at that time and nothing came from it.

At present many of the ablest minds are trying to devise expedients for preventing a repetition of the awful conflict which is only theoretically ended and the duration and main issues of which I have correctly predicted in an article printed in the *Sun* of December 20, 1914. The proposed League is not a remedy but on the contrary, in the opinion of a number of competent men, may bring about results just the opposite.It is particularly regrettable that a punitive policy was adopted in framing the terms of peace, because a few years hence it will be possible for nations to fight without armies, ships or guns, by weapons far more terrible, to the destructive action and range of which there is virtually no limit. A city, at any distance whatsoever from the enemy, can be destroyed by him and no power on earth can stop him from doing so. If we want to avert an impending calamity and a state of things which may transform this globe into an inferno, we should push the development of flying machines and wireless transmission of energy without an instant's delay and with all the power and resources of the nation.